Merlin R. Carothers

From
FEAR to
FAITH

Also by Merlin Carothers

Prison to Praise

Power in Praise

Answers to Praise

Praise Works!

Walking and Leaping

Bring Heaven into Hell

Victory on Praise Mountain

More Power to You

What's on Your Mind

Let Me Entertain You

Prison to Praise (the movie)

From FEAR *to* FAITH

MERLIN CAROTHERS

THOMAS NELSON PUBLISHERS
Nashville • Atlanta • London • Vancouver

Published in Nashville, Tennessee, by Thomas Nelson, Inc., Publishers, and distributed in Canada by Word Communications, Ltd., Richmond, British Columbia.

Unless otherwise noted, the Bible version used in this publication is THE NEW KING JAMES VERSION. Copyright © 1979, 1980, 1982, Thomas Nelson, Inc., Publishers. Verses marked TLB are taken from *The Living Bible,* copyright 1971 by Tyndale House Publishers, Wheaton, IL. Used by permission. Scripture quotations noted KJV are from the King James Version of the Bible. Scripture quotations noted AMPLIFIED are from THE AMPLIFIED BIBLE: Old Testament. Copyright © 1962, 1964 by Zondervan Publishing House (used by permission); and from THE AMPLIFIED NEW TESTAMENT. Copyright © 1958 by the Lockman Foundation (used by permission).

Library of Congress Cataloging-in-Publication Data

Carothers, Merlin R.
      From fear to faith / Merlin Carothers.
            p.   cm.
      ISBN 0-7852-7358-1 (pbk.)
      1. Providence and government of God. 2. Courage—Religious aspects—Christianity. 3. Carothers, Merlin R. I. Title.
BT135.C29 1997
241'.4—dc20
                                                                          96–36579
                                                                          CIP

Printed in the United States of America.
1 2 3 4 5 6 — 02 01 00 99 98 97

My special appreciation to my dear wife, Mary, who has edited, advised, and supported me in this book and everything I do. Her skill and spiritual wisdom have caused my work to be far better than I could have done alone.

Contents

CHAPTER 1

Controlled by Faith—Or by Fear?

We live by faith or by fear, and the one we choose makes all the difference in the world.

Do you have faith that God works in *all* the circumstances of your life for your good? Do you have faith that God gives you victory over your problems? Or do you fear that He is not that intimately involved in your life? If you want to move from fear to faith, or benefit from a stronger faith, I offer advice here on how to do that based on my experience in doing so.

God has provided me ample training in what it's like to be afraid. At the time I did not appreciate His methods, but now I see His careful attention to the details I needed to understand. I have learned that life is like a school; we must graduate from one grade in order to advance to the next. In this book I report a few of the classes that I was required to attend.

Walking through minefields during World War II really got my attention. Those times demonstrated to me that fear could cause me to perspire even in freezing temperatures! On one occasion when we were moving through the Black Forest in Germany at about one step per minute, we perspired so much that our clothing became soaking wet. In our training we had been repeatedly told how dangerous minefields were. Our reaction usually was, *I hear what you are saying, but it's not relevant—that will never happen to me.*

But seeing other men being blown apart by mines gave me justification to be terrified. Every time I put one foot on the ground I thought it might be my last step. At the time I had no understanding of how to have faith that God would take care of me. I had no perception that He wants to guide our steps.

Since those days, I don't believe I have ever walked through a forest without remembering the awesome marches. The memories cause every forest to be far more beautiful to me than if I had not seen the ravages of war. You are not apt to walk through military-style minefields, but similar conditions may lie ahead of you. I have written this book so you will be prepared. I pray that my journey will in some way prepare you to proceed on your exciting pilgrimage into higher levels of faith.

Fear and faith are powerful opposites. Fear destroys faith. Faith destroys fear.

A healthy, natural fear alerts us to danger and helps us live in our corrupted world. But when fear is exaggerated or misdirected, we suffer. We are robbed of faith, joy, strength, and possibly life. The Bible tells us 365 times not to be afraid. God wants to encourage us. He also wants us to know how dangerous fear can be.

Consider the human body. Reasonable fear protects us from foolishly putting ourselves at risk, but too much fear destroys the body. It can make the heart race, blood pressure rise, and cholesterol increase, and it can cause hundreds of internal reactions that may lead to sickness or death. That is simply the way God designed us.

Medical science says that if we spend years worrying that we will someday get a certain disease, fear could eventually create it. If we are ill, fear may prevent us from getting well.

God did not design us to be dominated by fear. I hope to convince you of something else: *God designed us with the ability to choose* **not** *to be controlled by fear.*

We are not helpless victims of the things we fear most: misfortune, pain, poverty, loneliness, ridicule, failure, or even death. Some will indeed happen, but the Scriptures tell us not to fear them. Fear may try to stalk us, but faith conquers it. And we have the power to choose the one by which we will live. If we abandon our faith in God, we become prey to the enemy of fear.

Fear whispers, "Yesterday was bad, today is horrible, and tomorrow will be worse. You can't do anything about it."

But in faith each of us can declare, "God was with me yesterday. He is with me today, and He will be with me forever. I can do all things through Christ, who gives me strength. Because of Him I live."

Fear causes us to retreat. We shrink back because we think our efforts will lead only to failure.

Faith encourages us to advance. We believe we can succeed, and we move boldly forward from triumph to triumph.

Fear causes us to turn away from spiritual battle until eventually we forget a battle is going on!

Faith helps us to do bold exploits for God.

Fear is an opiate. It drugs us into thinking we don't have to do what God would have us to do. It makes us relax in an easy chair and expect someone else to do what we ought to be doing. Fear can make us indifferent, apathetic, cowardly.

Faith enables us to know we *can* do something. Faith motivates and strengthens us. It stimulates, challenges, and gives us courage to persevere and overcome.

Fear can affect the way we feel; it can also contribute to the way we look and act. When fear controls us, we may look tense, angry, or depressed. When fear controls us, our troubles and trials seem too much to bear. Our shoulders are slumped. We feel terrible and we show it. Or we clench our teeth behind a mask of forced cheer, denying to ourselves and to others that fear exists.

In contrast, faith causes us to pull back our shoulders. Our steps are lighter. Whatever our troubles, they become a hundred times easier to bear. Believing that God loves us and works in everything that happens to us for our good causes the heart and mind to work better. High blood pressure goes down. Tense nerves relax. Attitudes change. We smile more. Whatever our circumstances, faith enables us to be joyful. We like ourselves and therefore become more likable. People respond better to people they like.

Joyous believing can cause us to

- be more successful.
- have new friends.
- have a better marriage.
- overcome feelings of inferiority.
- conquer bitterness and anger.
- overcome needless feelings of guilt.

The list is endless. The Bible declares, "Be strong in the Lord and in the power of His might" (Eph. 6:10).

I propose that we learn to be strong "in the power of His

— 4 —

might." If we choose to be weak, Satan can destroy us, our families, and all our resources!

Hundreds of books urge you to have more faith. But in this book I want to tell you *how* to have faith that gives you freedom from the fears that defeat you, brings answers to your prayers, and changes you.

I promise you that as you experience release from fear, you will have new pleasure in every hour of every day, new peace of mind, new excitement over the endless achievements you can enjoy. Fear may be the one factor that has prevented your faith from helping you accomplish the things you want to do.

We can permit faith or fear to control us. The choice is ours. In this book we will explore the workings of faith and fear, and how we can practice our faith to overcome fear. Let's discover together how we can live in faith and do it victoriously.

CHAPTER 2

The Smallest Seed

How strong is your desire to have faith that has power? Stories about other people's miraculous faith are encouraging, but it is far better to learn how faith works and how God designed it to do so.

For years I repeated certain prayers that accomplished nothing. I told God, other people, and myself that I believed a certain prayer had been answered. But in my heart I did not really believe that my problem was resolved. In my fifty years as a minister I have talked with and read letters from thousands who have had the same problem.

The solution is simple: *we must learn to believe!* That is, we must learn to believe in our hearts so we are no longer trying to fool our innermost thoughts. Let's be sure of one thing. We can never fool God; He always knows exactly what we believe:

> *You understand my thought afar off. . . .*
> *For there is not a word on my tongue,*
> *But behold, O LORD, You know it altogether* (Ps. 139:2–4).

You may be surprised to learn that we cannot fool ourselves, either. When we earnestly and sincerely try to believe what we really don't believe, we must remember that our bodies have complicated, sensitive, and intricately woven components, each seeming to "know" much about the others.

Consider the lie detector test. If you were tested and lied in response to a simple question such as, "Have you ever broken the speed limit?" it would register whether or not you told the truth. If you answered no, your body would react, "You just told a lie." Think of what your inner response would be if you were asked a very emotional question!

The conscious mind may not know exactly what is going on, but something inside does. The body functions something like a computer. If we entered 10,000 or even 1,000,000 correct keystrokes and one incorrect one for a complex mathematical formula on how to send a rocket to Mars, we may not get from the computer the response we seek. We could get angry, upset, or want to demolish the machine, but it would not respond until we corrected that one keystroke.

We can tell ourselves, others, and God that we believe in, trust in, and rely on Him, but if indeed we do not, something within us says, "You aren't telling the truth!" Proverbs 20:27 tells us that "the spirit of a man is the lamp of the LORD." He sees what we truly believe in our innermost hearts. If we understand this, then we won't be nearly so confused about some of our unanswered prayers.

I do not mean that God is saying, "I won't listen to you because you aren't doing it right." He knows our frailties. But we can't fool the innermost part of ourselves that knows exactly what we think and feel.

In Matthew 9:29, Jesus said, "According to your faith let it be to you." The opposite is equally true. Jesus could have said, "According to your fear let it be to you." He was saying that as we believe, so it is done. Therefore, it is imperative that we learn exactly how to believe and how to be delivered from fear.

My participation in World War II (as an infantry soldier in the Eighty-second Airborne Division), the Korean Conflict, and the Dominican Republic gave me many intense experiences in what it is like to be afraid.

In 1966 the army once again transported me from our relatively comfortable and safe environment in the U.S. to the Vietnam Conflict. During my 365 days in that agonizing war, I frequently visited men who had been severely injured when a truck or jeep ran over a mine. When I went to see them, I rode in a jeep through some of those same areas. I became intensely aware that I, too, might not leave Vietnam in one piece, and I had abundant reason to go from fear to even greater fear. If my faith had not grown, I would have become as fearful as some officers became. They simply avoided all possible danger, giving every conceivable excuse to stay as far as possible from harm's way.

As an army private in World War II, I went where I was told to go, but as a lieutenant colonel chaplain I went where I believed I *should* go. That required the strengthening of my faith. Would God protect me when I wasn't being forced to take such risks? I believed that He would.

We need to examine many aspects of the details we have stored within us. We may need to change one or more things about the persons we are. Then our faith is released in a new way. When we say, "I believe!" the "inner computer" runs a check. When everything comes out correctly, each part of the body and spirit cooperates to release God's joy, peace, and healing.

When a Christian says, "I have all the faith in the world, but God isn't answering my prayers," he is making opposite statements. When someone says, "God is not answering my prayers," he is also saying, "I do not believe God is answering."

When he says that God isn't answering his prayers, he is saying that God is doing exactly what he believes!

Sometimes our faith is crippled by our failure to pray within the boundaries of God's will. For example, it would be sheer folly to ask God to give us another person's spouse. And we should never attempt to pray against the rules and promises God has given us in His Word.

Once we realize how crucial it is to truly believe what we say, we will concentrate on learning to believe. We can learn!

The Power of a Seed

God created each of us with many abilities, one of which is the capacity to believe. Jesus told us to have faith as a mustard seed, which in His time was thought to be the smallest seed. He said to the disciples, "I say to you, if you have faith as a mustard seed, you will say to this mountain, 'Move from here to there,' and it will move; and nothing will be impossible for you" (Matt. 17:20).

The analogy was simple, yet so profound that it has often been misunderstood. Many Christians feel that Jesus was saying that even the smallest amount of faith could remove a mountain. He couldn't have meant that! Since He spoke those words, not one Christian, to the best of my knowledge, has ever had sufficient faith to remove a mountain by believing it would move. He was telling us that the nature of faith is like a seed; when cared for properly, it can grow. A grain of sand is perhaps larger than a mustard seed, but the sand will never increase in size.

Jesus never spoke sternly toward persons who had only a small amount of faith unless they had ample opportunities to grow in faith and refused to make the efforts.

He spoke harshly to the scribes and Pharisees who gloried in their own righteousness and knowledge of the Scripture but did not believe in Him as the promised Messiah. When the elders, chief priests, and the scribes asked Him if He was the Christ, He said, "If I tell you, you will by no means believe" (Luke 22:67).

When John the Baptist was suffering in prison, he sent two of his disciples to Jesus to ask Him, "Are You the Coming One, or do we look for another?" (Luke 7:20). Jesus patiently explained to John's followers how they could give John the comfort and assurance he needed: "Go and tell John the things you have seen and heard: that the blind see, the lame walk, the lepers are cleansed, the deaf hear, the dead are raised, the poor have the gospel preached to them" (Luke 7:22).

If you do not consider yourself a spiritual leader, but you do think of yourself as a fairly successful person, be aware that on one occasion Jesus spoke critically to a man who was classified only as a "nobleman." Jesus said to the nobleman, "Unless you people see signs and wonders, you will by no means believe" (John 4:48). Jesus honored the man's request but made it clear that faith *without* physical evidence should be our goal.

Jesus expected His disciple Thomas to have learned to have faith in Him, but Thomas could not believe that Jesus had been resurrected from the dead. Jesus said to him, "Thomas, because you have seen Me, you have believed. Blessed are those who have not seen and yet have believed" (John 20:29).

When Jesus addressed His disciples, He spoke to men who had listened to Him teach and had seen His many miracles yet still lacked the faith He thought they should have. In Matthew 17:17 Jesus was referring to His disciples when He said, "O faithless and perverse generation, how long shall I be with you? How long shall I bear with you?" These were indeed harsh words, but He thought these favored men should have learned something after the opportunities He had given them.

To Philip Jesus said, "Have I been with you so long, and yet you have not known Me, Philip? He who has seen Me has seen the Father; so how can you say, 'Show us the Father'?" (John 14:9).

Peter had actually walked on water, but he became afraid and sank. To him Jesus said, "O you of little faith, why did you doubt?" (Matt. 14:31).

If we have been Christians for years and still rest comfortably in our lack of faith, we need to reassess our progress and seek ways to go from fear to faith.

Some people teach that Christians should be immune to fear. I do not believe that is true. We are all subject to fears of one kind or another. But we can *learn how to be delivered* from whatever fear has invaded our minds. My own faith is far smaller than I would like it to be, but I am determined to do whatever I can to help it grow. And I've learned that if I patiently endure every painful circumstance and believe that God is always working for my good (Rom. 8:28), my faith steadily increases. What about your faith? Is it also increasing?

If you are living in a painful situation, you can now begin to trust and believe that God is working for your good. You can claim this promise for your past, present, and all future situations. Romans 12:12 gives us a marvelous way to deal with the future: "Be glad for all God is planning for you" (TLB).

Jesus likened faith to the tiny mustard seed that grew until it produced a bush that might reach as high as eight feet. Its branches often were large enough to use as wood. Like the seed, our faith can and will grow if we give it a chance. When it matures, nothing is impossible.

It takes six to eight years for the mustard seed to grow into an eight-foot bush. If it does not reach its full height in a day, a month, or a year, would the wise farmer dig it up and throw it away as useless? No. Faith is supposed to grow in the same way—gradually.

If we reject our faith because we feel it is not eight feet tall, we will never know the power of faith that changes us and the world around us. Jesus did not belittle anyone's faith, no matter how small. He praised the kind of faith that was growing.

Faith that works must be nurtured hour by hour, day by day. How is faith nurtured? By choosing to believe that it is there and growing, even when you don't feel it. But you may ask, "How do I know that I have a seed of faith to begin with?" In Romans 12:3, Paul wrote, "God has dealt to each one a measure of faith."

Faith is a gift, not something we have deserved or worked up for ourselves. Some Christians labor under the delusion that either we believe or we don't believe. In reality we believe in varying degrees.

Growth is in the nature of a seed. Not only does God plant the seed of faith in our hearts, but He also tells us how to encourage its growth. The writer of Hebrews 12:2 tells us to look "unto Jesus, the author and finisher of our faith."

A seed can't make itself grow; it needs sun and rain. But that is not all it needs. The farmer must also cultivate the soil. He knows well the truth of James 2:20: "Faith without works is dead."

God gives you and me faith, but it will not grow unless we learn how to cultivate it. Without cultivation it could remain as a tiny seed during our entire lives.

Steps to Faith

If we get up grouchy in the morning, hurry off to work where we give little thought to God or His will, hurry home to relax by the television, then read a few verses of Scripture before retiring, we will have little opportunity for our faith to grow.

Somehow we all must find a way to begin each day with a spiritual exercise that causes our faith to grow. An example would be to read or quote Scriptures (there are many in this book) emphasizing the victory that we have in Christ.

Whatever we elect to do, we need to do it nearly 365 days a year. Otherwise we soon discover that we seldom, or never, do it. Consistency is a key.

I've been told that it takes twenty minutes of vigorous exercise for the body to circulate and cleanse all of its blood. Spiritual exercise also requires time.

Years ago I began going for a walk the first thing every morning. As I walk up the steep hill near our home, I concentrate on hearing whatever the Holy Spirit wants to tell me. For about a year, those early morning walks required much discipline. I could always think of a good reason why I should skip my spiritual exercise for that day. Now, I feel disappointed if something prevents me from having that special time with God. I urgently need it to learn how I can be used by God to build His kingdom.

Jesus knew by age twelve that it was important for Him to be engaged in His Father's business. His teachings urge us to follow His example.

The disciples asked Jesus, "What shall we do, that we may work the works of God?" And He answered, "This is the work of God, that you believe in Him whom He sent" (John 6:28–29).

Our job is to believe. We experience new spiritual strength as our faith increases.

Jesus selected a mountain as the object to be moved by faith. Why? Because of its immense size. By selecting a mountain,

Jesus was saying, "By your faith you can defeat the biggest problems that can ever come into your life."

A dry seed cannot crack a solid rock. But as that seed grows, it can split the rock.

A huge rock beside our home was about twenty-five feet long and twenty feet wide. Long ago a pine tree seed had fallen into a tiny crevice and grown to about fifty feet high. In the process it split the great rock.

In the same way, faith, while still the size of a mustard seed, will not move a mountain-sized problem. Yet as it grows, it will. This gives us all hope. No matter how difficult our problem, we can find a solution if we have faith.

If you encountered an enormous "mountain" such as life-threatening cancer, a mustard seed–sized faith could not instantly remove it. You may have observed people striving to believe that God had healed a cancer. But if their faith was still the size of a mustard seed, they became discouraged.

That is why we need situations that nurture our faith. If God in His love gives us opportunities to mature in our faith, we should face each problem with joy. We can learn to persistently and patiently declare that in each and every situation He is working all things for our good.

Lessons in the Sky

When I was thirteen years old, I knew I wanted to someday fly an airplane. For years I took every opportunity to closely observe any airplane on the ground, and I never failed to longingly gaze at every one that I saw in the air. That flying airplanes might be dangerous didn't enter my mind, but a couple of incidents in the military educated me quickly.

During World War II, I was a passenger on a military aircraft that was over the ocean and on fire. Would the gas tanks explode? Would we crash, or would we be able to get into life rafts? We were all frightened, and I remember hearing some men praying.

The pilot shut off one of the two engines and put the plane into a dive in an effort to extinguish the fire. He was able to put out the flames and made it to land on one engine. How frightened was I? Exceedingly!

When we exited the plane, we sat along a small isolated dirt runway until trucks arrived to take us to our destination. The pilot never bothered to tell us privates what had happened. Perhaps he needed permission because of our mission.

Years later, as an army chaplain, I visited a pilot who had crashed into the flagpole at the post headquarters. I don't know if they ever learned why he was flying so low. In his hospital bed he looked horrible. He was in a coma and was being kept alive by several machines. As I stood beside his corpselike body, the thought came to me, *Do I really want to fly airplanes?* If I had given in to those fears, I would have missed the many years that I enjoyed flying. Now I rejoice that God gave me opportunities to be afraid and opportunities to grow in faith that He would protect me.

You may ask, "But what about Christian pilots who crashed? Why didn't God protect them?" It is my conviction that if they were being reasonably cautious, they were scheduled to be with the Lord on that day. Death could have happened while they were driving an automobile, or they could have had a heart attack. When or how we die is not as important as our learning to go from fear to faith.

Each day your faith can grow a little stronger. You may not see it growing, just as you cannot measure a mustard seed's growth after one day. However, daily growth produces results.

You may never have a mountain-sized problem in your life, but it is very likely that someone you know will need extra help. As you exercise the faith you do have, it will grow and grow. Then you will be ready to give that extra help. God's Word tells us that our faith will overcome the world. No mountain-sized problem is large enough to overwhelm or defeat us: "This is the victory that has overcome the world—our faith" (1 John 5:4).

When faith does not produce instant, visible results, too many Christians want to quit. They may understand faith to mean, "Pray, and receive an immediate answer."

With no apparent miracle, some folks feel that God is not answering their prayers. Fear then overcomes their faith. If a little mustard plant is plucked from the earth and not replanted, it dies. No amount of sunshine and water can help it. That's the way God designed it. He can and will permit things to happen in our lives that have the potential to cause our faith to die. Why does He allow these things to happen? Because He knows that if we choose to respond in faith, our small faith will grow larger and stronger. Our part is to nurture the mustard-seed faith He gave us—day by day, year by year—for as long as He permits. Our quiet determination is a joy to God. He may allow people or circumstances to knock us down, but only to help us learn that faith can work and grow in us.

Speaking of being knocked down, I once had the experience of being forced down. While flying a small airplane with no radio, I became totally lost. No matter in which direction I looked, nothing on the ground looked anything like the map I was trying to follow. The sun had set and darkness was falling. It was my first long-distance flight, over completely new territory, and I didn't know what to do. My instructor had taught me, "If you become lost, look for a safe place to land." But I was over a city. No place seemed to be a safe place to land.

After I circled round and round for a while, trying to get my bearings, I decided to go in the general direction of my destination and hope for the best. Darkness was coming more rapidly than it had come in my entire life! Was I afraid? No doubt about it; I was scared. God must have smiled. He saw that Merlin was being prepared to understand what it's like to be afraid. Maybe He thought, *If Merlin is going to write a book someday about fear, he needs to understand what it's like.*

Here at my desk it's easy for me to think, *Why was I afraid? God was taking care of me.* But at the time it wasn't very clear to me how intimately God is involved in our lives.

In a few minutes something happened that made me even more afraid. Suddenly two high-speed military aircraft buzzed around me. Their maneuvers made it mandatory for me to go in the direction they were herding me. They forced me to what I soon realized was a landing strip. Seeing the safe landing place was a comfort, but I knew something bad was happening. I had never been forced to land a plane, and I hadn't heard of anyone having that experience.

When my plane came to a complete stop, I saw military police vehicles racing toward me with the lights flashing. Since I, too, was in the army, I knew something was wrong. It was. I had been flying over Fort Knox! The people who guard all that gold didn't like unidentified planes flying over them.

What a stern lecture I received! They told me they were authorized to shoot down unauthorized aircraft. I expected them to put handcuffs on me and march me away. But after they had examined my plane, saw I had no radio, and examined my flying logbook, they realized I was a poor lost pilot. The next morning they made sure I knew how to find my way home and sent me on my way. God provided me with a problem, let me perspire a little, and then supplied His solution.

I'm convinced that my experiences were designed to show me how little faith I had and how much I needed to trust that God was involved in things that happened to me. I don't mean that He always causes bad things to happen just so He can teach us something. I mean that He causes us to be where we need to be so that we can learn what we need to learn.

I was once on a troop ship that was being attacked by a German submarine in the middle of the Atlantic Ocean. All of my "fun" experiences seem to have happened at night. The anxious captain had us on the deck so we could more quickly get into lifeboats. I can still picture the black, foreboding sea, and I remember how frightened we all were. The thought of the ship's going down and our being cast into the sea got my attention, and that was all God had in mind for the time being.

We know that God could solve all our problems and change everything with a sweep of His hand, but that isn't His plan. He wants us to believe and continue to believe and believe some more. What would a little mustard plant do if someone stepped on it? It would strive a little harder to reach back toward the sky. That is the way our faith grows. Paul spoke proudly of the believers in Thessalonica for "patience and faith in all your persecutions and tribulations" (2 Thess. 1:4).

Practice Believing

Jesus knew that as we practiced believing, we would nurture our faith, which in turn would produce joy and spiritual strength. To His followers who would not believe, He said, "O ye slow of heart, why will you not believe?" (Luke 24:25, author's paraphrase). He was saddened that humans would reject the seed of faith and the capacity to grow in believing that He placed within us.

I am not certain how faith works its mysterious ways, but I believe we can observe some things about it.

First, *when we practice believing, the gifts God has given us are activated.* Paul wrote to Timothy, "Stir up the gift of God which is in you" (2 Tim. 1:6). The exercise of faith activates all other gifts. Our task is to stir up our faith into action!

Second, *as we use the faith that we have, God adds to it.* The parable of the talents shows us that God gives us even more when we use what He has already given us. Jesus told His disciples, "For whoever has, to him more will be given" (Matt. 13:12). Every time our faith grows, God will give us more.

Third, *God acts sovereignly—completely separate from our faith.* He works His eternal purposes not because of our level of faith, but because He is God. At those times, the initiative is His, not ours.

Since He is infinitely greater than our ability to understand Him, we can't comprehend all the whys and hows of His mysterious ways. He gives us simple directions, and our task is to trust and obey. God sometimes acts sovereignly, apart from our faith, but He wants us to use the faith we have. In Hebrews 11:6, we read, "Without faith it is impossible to please Him."

It is in learning how to believe that we receive God's blessings and the ability to do His will. Sometimes educated men and women find that simple, childlike faith is the most difficult thing to accomplish. God knows when our faith is weak, but He wants us to take the faith we do have and use it.

What if the mustard seed expected to be fully grown after only one day? What if it worked with all its might for an entire year and still wasn't fully grown? What if each day it measured itself and said, "See, I haven't grown even one inch; it would be wrong of me to call myself a mustard plant. I'll never be of any use!" Exercising the small amount of faith that we have is not wrong. Our failure to believe is wrong. Unbelief is the willful refusal to believe. That kept the Israelites from entering the promised land.

Paul did not mince words in Romans 14:23 when he wrote, "Whatever is not from faith is sin." Using our faith opens our hearts to what faith can do. That is why Satan has worked so hard to keep us from learning. He wants the seed of faith to lie dormant in us, never to grow. But God has planted faith in us, and He will cause it to grow when we trust in Him. This truth is our best defense against the lies of our enemy Satan. In Ephesians 6:16, Paul wrote, "Above all, taking the shield of faith."

Jesus knew that it took a mustard seed years to grow into a mature, productive plant. He could have told us to have faith like a grain of wheat that produces a mature plant in one short season. Or He could have compared our faith to a tiny seed hidden in the cone of a cedar of Lebanon that requires seventy years to reach its towering height. Instead, He spoke of faith as a mustard seed. He doesn't ask unreasonable things of us. What may seem difficult, even impossible at times, becomes possible, even reasonable, with Christ who is the author and finisher of our faith. We can trust that our faith is growing if we give it a chance.

I'm convinced that we can hasten death if we fail to learn more about trusting God. On one occasion I nearly met my Maker because I was afraid. A friend loaned me some underwater scuba-diving equipment. I had always wanted to swim underwater without having to come up every minute to get air, but I had never before had the opportunity. All my friend knew about the equipment was to tell me how to put it on. He knew nothing about the dangers involved, so he didn't know enough to tell me how careful I should be. With no fear I plunged into the Atlantic Ocean. Just as I expected, it was exciting and amazing. There I was—swimming with the fish.

Something happened to the breathing apparatus. Suddenly there was no oxygen. I had to get to the surface quickly! Then it hit me—panic. With overwhelming fear I raced upward. When I hit the surface, I gulped for air and managed to get both air and water into my lungs. Then I tried to get the air tank off my back so I could stay afloat, but it was more difficult to get off than it had been to put it on while I was on dry land. For seemingly endless minutes I thrashed about and realized that the tank was going to weigh me down. Fear seemed to wipe out my ability to think clearly.

Needless to say, I survived. How, I'm not quite sure, but what a quick, violent lesson I received about the power of fear. Now as I look back I see that my loving Father was merely giving me more free instruction on the importance of living in faith rather than in fear.

Faith does not change God's mind. He already knows what we need. Faith changes the person who is doing the believing. We should pray and believe—keep on praying and keep on believing that our faith is growing and that we are being changed into the image of Christ. With His faith growing in us, how can we fail?

Jude wrote, "But you, beloved, building yourselves up on your most holy faith" (Jude 20). Faith is alive in you. Choose to believe, and watch it grow.

One of the most exciting times of my day is during my early morning prayer walk. I practice believing that I'm receiving everything God has available for me right then. That my heart and lungs are working better, my bones are being made stronger, my entire body is singing with new health through the gifts Jesus provides to me. With each step I believe that something good is being accomplished in me.

Most of all, I practice believing that God's Holy Spirit is working in my spirit and in my soul to cleanse me, inspire me, make me a better servant, give me more zeal, strengthen my mind, and help me to love Him more and to love people more. After a while I feel in my spirit that I'm experiencing the mounting up on wings like an eagle that Isaiah wrote about.

My prayer for you, as you continue to read, is that you will believe that your faith is growing. In the next chapter we look at the nature of our fears. As we learn to banish them, our faith continues to grow stronger.

CHAPTER 3

The Specter of Fear

Fear lurks in the silent darkness. Unwanted—hated—yet even when ignored or denied, it can control our destiny. The first time I made a parachute jump I was afraid. I had been vigorously indoctrinated to believe I was a fearless paratrooper, too courageous to be frightened.

Emerson wrote, "Do the thing you fear and the death of fear is certain." This is often true, but in my second jump I was still afraid. I didn't know it then, but my lessons in living and coping with the more insidious aspects of fear had just begun. I had much to learn about fear's enormous capacity to influence behavior.

In 1943, we arrived at Fort Benning, Georgia: two hundred robust, cocky volunteers in the famed U.S. Army Paratroops. We were from all over the United States, we had completed infantry basic training, and we were confident that we were the elite of the army. We could do anything. Physical tests taken before coming to Benning had, we thought, separated the men from the boys. We were ready to show the army some real men.

Afraid? Never! It was a new adventure.

The sergeants who greeted us knew our attitudes. They had been where we were. As experts, they were ready and eager to pulverize our egos. At the bus terminal they swooped down on us like sharks with minnows.

"Pick up those bags, you chicken-livered mamas' boys, and let's go."

Mamas' boys? Sergeant, you don't know who you're talking to. We aren't afraid of you or anyone else!

How wrong we were.

The sergeants had one objective—to separate the men from the boys. In their something-less-than-humble opinion, the men were those who would never give up regardless of injury, suffering, or torture.

In infantry basic training we had learned to run, or so we thought. But at Airborne School we never went for a run. All we ever did was run, run, and run. Anytime we moved it was on the run. We ran to the latrine. We ran to chow. To training sites—five, ten, or more miles—we ran. Finally we reached the level of fitness at which we could run for hours on end without tiring. Failing meant, heaven forbid, being transferred out of the glorious Airborne.

But running was fun compared with the rigors at training sites. At one of them, we were suspended from harnesses like those that would connect us to a parachute when we would descend from plane to ground. The straps, holding our dead weight and digging into our groins, felt like thin wires straining under two hundred pounds of agonized flesh.

We hung in those harnesses while sergeants explained the fine art of being a "famous paratrooper."

"Do you hurt, mamas' boys? Want to quit?"

Quit? No way!

The worst thing that could happen to a sergeant was to have one of the mamas' boys freeze in the airplane—not ready to leap into space. Their plan was to weed out every trainee who had the potential to quit. The earlier the better. We were convinced the sergeants got a bonus for every one they could make a washout. No one wanted to quit, but the sergeants, it seemed, had stronger wills. After the first week our group of 200 had decreased to 150 stalwarts.

Before each washout departed, we were lined up by the truck that would take him to some unknown, abominable site for a truly awful assignment. The sergeants led us in jeering the miserable failure. The harsh tactic was used to make those of us who remained that much more determined not to be quitters and never to be afraid.

At the end of the second week, 125 champions remained. We ended preliminary training, acutely aware that the lowest we could ever sink was to be a washout. So far, so good. We were fearless; we were the aristocracy of the elite. At least that's what we wanted to believe. On the morning of our first jump, our barracks echoed with jubilant shouts of "Geronimo!"

The worst was yet to come.

That evening we returned in triumph to the barracks, brimming with gusto. We had made it! We were veterans, almost. Not quite full-fledged paratroopers until we had made five jumps—earning the coveted Parachute Wings—but we were on our way.

We noticed that our number had shrunk from 125 to 120. Where were the others? We learned that they had been injured. One had a broken leg, but he would recover. One had a broken back, we were told. In training, no one had mentioned that possibility.

The next morning we were a bit less enthused about our upcoming jump. Everyone tried to show bravado, but none of us could forget the man with the broken back. A sergeant lined us up for another lecture: "Yesterday one of this group of stupid little boys failed to do what he was taught. He will not jump again. While preparing to land he was so scared that he looked down at the ground rather than straight ahead as you were all taught. He broke his back. If anyone else wants a broken back, do the same thing."

That evening several more of our comrades failed to return. Fear set in. Our chosen occupation wasn't all fun and games. Two men went AWOL. They couldn't face the humiliation of the quitters' parade.

In our fourth jump, three men froze in fear at the open door of the plane, refusing to make the plunge into space. They were treated with the most disdain of all. That evening they were paraded before us, derided as "the most contemptible examples of cowards that three mothers ever brought into the world." The rest of us vowed that we would never permit ourselves to be so vilified.

The morning of our fifth jump, there was an oppressive silence in our barracks. If anyone had asked, "Are you afraid?" we would have shot back, "Afraid? No!" We would have been sincere. Each of us reasoned, "I haven't quit. Therefore, I'm not afraid." The quitters had been afraid. However, if an animal with a keen sense of smell had been nearby, it would easily have detected the fear that we stubbornly denied.

I made it through the five qualifying jumps without a scratch. Afraid? Yes, indeed. But I had learned to deny fear, and like the others, I stood triumphantly as our commanding general pinned the silver wings on my chest. We were now in the army's most elite society of warriors. No reason to be afraid—that is, not until our next leap into space.

More Lessons to Learn

My lessons in fear had not ended. There was more, much more, to learn. We were told of openings in specialist schools.

Communications School? At nineteen that seemed too dull. Demolitions School? Now *that* sounded exciting! This misguided private volunteered.

There I met with an entirely different kind of fear. Training sergeants told us explicitly what various explosives could do to the human body. They wanted us to be afraid, but then instructed us to control our fear and not let it control us. We could not do the required delicate work if our hands shook with fear. Several men's hands trembled as they tried to arm bombs set to explode. They were disqualified.

My paratrooper training had convinced me that I was a man of steel. I had to prove I had nerves of steel. I stood alone on a training field holding several pounds of plastic explosives. The sergeant asked me to demonstrate the skills we had learned. If I failed, there would be no graduation ceremony for me!

After Demolitions School, and the disastrous detours described in my first book, *Prison to Praise*, I was assigned to combat duty as an infantry soldier with the Eighty-second Airborne Division. My next seven parachute jumps were in Europe where I had many chances to practice denying and controlling my fears. During my time in combat, I wished many times that "demolitions expert" was not on my record. At times my hands shook with fear, despite telling myself that I alone determined if and when the explosives ignited. I learned how fear can dominate everything we do.

Battle of the Bulge

The sergeant repeated it a second time: "You are to take the point position tonight. Keep your eyes and ears open. We expect panzers are heading our way."

It dawned on me that I would be alone in a foxhole, out in front of the entire U.S. Army. Fear began to take hold. I knew that if the German Army attacked that night, there would be nothing between me and their dreaded panzers. I'd be the first Allied soldier they would run into. Or run over.

It was late December 1944. The Allies reeled from the fierce counteroffensive the Germans had launched through the Ardennes Forest of Belgium. It would be known as the Battle of the Bulge.

My division, the Eighty-second Airborne, had been forced several times to pull back. Foot soldiers were no match for tanks. According to a 1953 U.S. Army statistical report, 19,246 American men were killed in action, suffered fatal wounds, or died while being held prisoner in that one Ardennes campaign. More than 62,000 men received nonfatal wounds, making it the heaviest single battle toll in U.S. history. British Prime Minister Winston Churchill called it the greatest American battle of the war.

The Germans used tanks to good advantage, and they seemingly had an endless supply. Those they sent to fight us were the biggest and best they had.

As I headed out beyond the last line of U.S. infantry, I had reason to be afraid. That other Americans would be in foxholes behind me was no comfort. I would have felt better with American tanks coming to the rescue.

I was in A Company, 508th Airborne Infantry Regiment, Eighty-second Airborne, one of the army's elite divisions, and we felt we were the best. But I wasn't feeling particularly brave at the time.

At my designated position I dug in; my only protection was a foxhole. No one had to say "dig deeper, soldier." I had a trusty M1 rifle and a few antitank grenades that I lined up before me. My rifle would shoot straight, but grenades seldom went where you aimed them.

As night fell, I waited in my foxhole for I knew not what. I was *really* afraid.

Why did the sergeant choose me for the point position? That was jargon for putting someone in front of everyone else in a maneuver, so only one soldier gets shot. A kind of trip wire. Who wants to be point man? Nobody. Aside from sounding an alarm, what was I expected to do in a panzer attack? I didn't feel capable of turning back one tank, let alone hundreds. I was on guard duty, supposed to stay alert to detect any signs of attack. I had no illusions about becoming a hero. My primary desire was to get out of the war alive and in one piece.

Listening to the wind and rustling trees, I thought they sounded like panzers. I shook my head and tried to think of something else. I tried to enjoy the moonlight glistening off the snow, but that lasted only a little while. Then I imagined that German soldiers were crawling silently toward me. The glistening was probably from piano wire that would be used to strangle me. I shuddered.

The rest of the night was more of the same. My fear of the panzers haunted me, though I tried to keep it at bay. I was practicing the fine art of being afraid.

An old army saying goes: "There are no atheists in foxholes." That was true for me that night. Except for a brief time in my youth, I hadn't had much use for God. In the foxhole, I cried out to Him to help me not be afraid.

Seeing an enemy tank headed right at you is an awesome experience. Talk about fear! That's the moment to be afraid.

But seeing a friendly tank, out in front of you with its guns pointed at the enemy, is a thoroughly different experience. That tank is working *for* you—for your good.

When you think of your difficulties as something like an

enemy tank, you are afraid. That's when you need a totally new perspective.

God can cause our problems to work *for* us. If we trust Him, He will turn them around, facing the enemy, and make them work for our good. Once we see that picture clearly and believe God is working, we will have the joy of seeing Him accomplish many good things in us. As we trust God to work for our good, He will eventually release incredible joy inside us.

Morning dawned. The panzers had not come. I had survived being on point. In the haze I saw twelve of our soldiers move off to my right. They were advancing! I was less afraid, and I thought, *Great, now there will be someone else between those panzers and me!* Then I saw an entire company of American soldiers right behind the first group. As some 150 men advanced, my muscles relaxed for the first time in hours.

Then I saw a sight that really warmed my heart. A column of our Sherman tanks moved toward the front. I thought it might be part of General Patton's Third Army. He was a formidable fighter, one of our heroes. If his army was involved, I thought we might get out alive. The clanking and rumbling of the tanks were music to my ears.

The Battle of the Bulge was in 1944–45; when I look back at that episode in my life, I marvel at how God used it to teach me some very important lessons. While in the Battle of the Bulge, I was also in a personal battle, whether I would be controlled by fear or by faith. I began to see that both faith and fear are common in life, but they are powerful enemies and opposing spiritual forces. It is a spiritual law that fear breeds lack of confidence and produces defeat. Yet it is equally a spiritual law that faith breeds confidence and victory.

Fear is like an army of enemy tanks that threatens us and makes us cower. Faith is like an army of friendly tanks that protects and allows us to advance victoriously. In this light, have you ever felt as if an army was out there waiting for a chance to squash you, to grind you down in your foxhole? If you have, I know how you feel.

Chaplain Carothers

I returned to the army as a chaplain in 1953, with good reasons to no longer be afraid. I believed the promise of 1 John 4:18 that "perfect love casts out fear." But I was still very much afraid to jump out of a perfectly good airplane while in flight.

As airborne chaplain, I made seventy-eight additional jumps. Men who carefully followed instructions usually broke no bones, although we always hit the ground with a jolt. After the parachute jumps, I would go to the hospital to visit the men who had been injured. Only a few of those who jumped were seriously hurt, but their injuries grieved me deeply. And it didn't help my battle with fear.

My injuries didn't quiet my fears, either. Part of me believed we were protected by hosts of angels whose primary duty was to ensure that paratroopers lived to jump another day. The first inkling that my angel might be off duty was when I made a two-point landing—feet first, then on my head. I managed to roll up my chute, carry it off the field, and sit under a tree. It took two hours to recall where I was and realize I had made another parachute jump.

On two occasions I was knocked out on impact with the ground. Other landings in trees, in ditches, in water, and on rocks convinced me that parachuting can be dangerous.

Night jumps held gut-gripping terror for those of us who were halfway sane. We sat in bucket seats until the jumpmaster said, "Stand up." Our static lines were hooked behind us without the security of seeing ourselves attached to anything.

Interior lights were turned off so our eyes would adapt to outside blackness.

At the right of the rear-exit doors was a red light about the size of a quarter, looking forebodingly evil. Every eye was on it. When it went out, a green one came on, meaning "go!" Not "go if you feel like it." Not "go if you aren't afraid." It meant "swallow your terror and leap out into the dark void."

Then came the plunge into black space, the air shrieking past our ears, into the bottomless pit of darkness. For seconds that seemed endless, we were gripped in a fist of pure force. The prop-blast flung us like cannonballs into the night. We tumbled through blackness until we reached the end of the unyielding static line attached to the plane. Wham! One instant we were going one way and the next we were reversed with a violent jerk.

Will the chute open? was the paratroopers' fear as we were thrust into space. Once it opened there was no sensation of falling; we felt suspended utterly alone in space as Planet Earth seemed to rush to meet us with a crushing embrace.

If you see ground before landing, you can soften the impact with a sudden strong pull on the four risers about twenty-five feet above ground, releasing them just before you crash-land. Air is momentarily trapped in the chute, and you may make a soft landing. But with the old World War II chute, it was more like jumping from your car at thirty miles an hour. The approaching earth was not the greatest fear; it gives a little. But rocks, trees, or buildings could give you broken bones or worse.

Why would anyone ever face these dangers if not absolutely necessary? Men seem to have a desire to prove their bravery, and I was no exception. I went on jumping, despite the ever-present fear in my ninety leaps into infinity. I am grateful for the valuable lessons on how to cope—and how not to—with fear.

As a paratrooper I learned to deal with fear by denying it, hoping it would go away. I tried to hide my emotions, telling myself and others I wasn't afraid, but that didn't help much as long as I was really afraid.

As a demolitions expert I learned that fear was not to be denied, but controlled. My survival and that of others often depended on my ability to act as though I was not afraid, even in the grip of terror. I spent all the energy and willpower I could muster to do that. I was being permeated by fear that threatened to control me.

As a chaplain I knew that God's influence was more powerful than the apprehension I fought when I jumped from a plane. Still, fear darkened my spirit and clutched at my guts, mocking my faith. Why couldn't I shake it? I would return from a jump emotionally exhausted from an inward battle. Fighting the fear had drained me.

You may live in a situation that often brings fear into your heart, and you may be doing your best to persevere, but fear and frustration persist. Since my parachute-jumping days, I have learned things I wish I'd known long ago.

Learning to Defeat Fear

It began as I learned to praise and thank God for all the circumstances in my life, the difficult as well as the good. As I thanked Him for things I feared most, an amazing thing began to happen; the fears subsided. Slowly it dawned on me: *there is a way to conquer fear. We can learn how to be delivered from its insidious power.* I had taken the first step when I could thank God for my fear instead of in spite of it. As long as I fought it by denying or controlling it, I was in its power. When I admitted being afraid and thanked God for the circumstances and my own helplessness, the opposite of what I expected happened. Instead of being engulfed by terror, the power of fear was broken, and the thing I feared was much less formidable.

It is a curious paradox that as long as we fight fear, it is victorious and remains our tormentor. But when we meet it with gratitude and faith, it is defeated and in fact becomes our ally.

In the next chapter I discuss how to take authority over our fears. God has, step by step, taught me the *how*. It's been a sometimes painful but wonderfully exciting journey to gain freedom from fear.

CHAPTER 4

Authority over Fear

The apostle Paul was not afraid of a scorpion. His lack of fear caused people who had never heard about Jesus to become interested in everything Paul had to say. Paul was convinced that animals, even poisonous ones, could not harm him (Acts 28:3–6). However, when I was taking the jungle expert course in Panama, I did not understand that I had any authority over fear.

We were walking through a dense tangle of vines and tropical shrubs that completely obliterated the sky. There was no path, so we had to use machetes to make our way through the undergrowth. Then it happened—so quickly that I didn't have even a second to prepare—a twelve-foot snake dropped from the trees right in front of my face! I had never seen a snake that was longer than three feet, and my heart immediately recognized that it lived in a body that was terrified. It seems strange now, but I was too frightened to make a sound or to move. The snake looked me in the eye, decided it didn't want me for lunch, and went on its way.

While I was enduring the jungle training and other similar schooling, I had no idea that God would use these events to prepare me for two unexpected events:

1. Being selected to go to Vietnam, where the temperature and the humidity were both ninety-seven!

2. Being selected to be promoted to lieutenant colonel on the 5 percent list. The army is permitted by Congress to promote up to a maximum of 5 percent of its officers who do not have sufficient time-in-grade to be considered. Getting promoted is a big thing in an officer's life. Some men spend thirty years dreaming of making the coveted 5 percent list, but it never occurred to me that I would ever be considered. To my knowledge no chaplain had ever been on the list, and I assumed that we were excluded from consideration.

When my name appeared on the list, it seemed to me that God must have written it in when no one was looking. But perhaps the rigorous training had something to do with it.

I mention these experiences to illustrate that God will go to any length to prepare us for our next assignment. Some things are difficult, and others are delightful. He knows the correct balance to prepare His servants for the best use.

In so many unconventional ways, God has helped me understand how faith can overcome fears. What I have learned has not given me any quick, easy solutions, but God has convinced me that fear of any kind can be eliminated by faith.

The Smell of Fear

A dog knows when a person is afraid of him. He smells the distinct aroma of fear.

As pastor of a church in Escondido, California, I gave a sermon on taking authority over our fears, and I used an illustration of how to confront an angry dog. The very next day a member had a chance to practice what he learned. A neighbor had left a water hose turned on, and it was flooding both their yards. Efforts to alert the people next door failed, so Jim climbed the fence between the yards. He turned the water off and was heading back when he heard a scurrying noise and an angry snarl. The neighbor's newly acquired Doberman pinscher, fangs bared, charged toward him.

Jim froze, then remembered my sermon. He stepped toward the dog, pointed his finger, and shouted, "Down!" The dog obeyed.

Keeping an eye on him, Jim again started toward the fence. When the Doberman saw him retreat, it leaped up and charged again. Jim again forcefully commanded, "Down!" and once more the animal obeyed. That time Jim made it to the top of the fence before the dog dashed toward him. The racket alerted the neighbor's wife, who came running from the house. From his perch on the fence, my friend told her what had occurred.

She exclaimed, "Oh, my gosh! He's a trained guard dog and has bitten several people!" My friend was thankful for learning one benefit of taking authority over fear.

We who believe and trust in God have the ability to examine the source of our fears and combat them. We can use the tools that God has given us.

In my paratrooper days I tried in vain to take authority over my fears by denying, controlling, or fighting them. I may have seemed to be in charge of them, but they were always there to haunt me. Though I tried to insist I wasn't afraid, I didn't even believe myself. My fears did not go away, no matter how forcefully I took control.

A trained dog will not respond to a command from someone who doubts his own authority to give it. Dog trainers must train owners as well. My friend who commanded his neighbor's dog to lie down had become convinced by my words the day before that the dog would accept his authority.

So, in taking authority over our fears, we must have faith that God has given us authority over them. We are told in James 4:7 to "submit to God. Resist the devil and he will flee from you."

But we are not told to close our eyes and pretend there is no devil. Or no snarling dog. Or no fear. The dog was real. It would be natural to be afraid. But when we understand something about the nature of dogs, and the authority we can have over them, we are able to use it. In Christ we have been given authority over our fears. Knowing something about the nature of our fears and our God-given authority over them frees us to use that power.

Some fears turn out to be completely unfounded or imaginary. Once we know the facts, our fear dissipates. It is like turning on the light in a room that held the terror of darkness.

Such was my inordinate teenage fear of girls. Throughout high school I often saw young ladies I wanted to date. I would walk toward one I saw as especially attractive, but at the last minute turn away. On the football field I never thought of being afraid, but a romantic approach toward a girl brought terror. Even in my first year of college my tongue still failed me in expressing interest in a female classmate.

Once a friend arranged for me to escort a young coed to a banquet. She was beautiful, seen by many as the most sought-after girl on campus. She was sixteen and I seventeen. I was nervous.

I arrived at the women's dormitory to pick up my date, and I waited, pacing nervously. Then, there she was gliding toward me, smiling, graceful in her dazzling evening gown. I fumbled with my tie. My face grew warm. I was speechless, and I had to remind myself to breathe. I managed a smile and awkward greeting; then, curiously light-headed, I escorted my first beauty queen to the banquet.

Through the evening I rehearsed over and over how I would invite her to go out with me again, but when I opened my mouth, my tongue seemed paralyzed. At school year's end, I went off to World War II and never again got the courage to ask for a date with my campus queen. Later I learned that she had been interested in me for what she saw as my intense spiritual zeal. How foolish I had been to allow fear to control my actions! My fears were imaginary and carried no real threats.

I remember when my shyness toward girls left me. I walked down Main Street in Beaver Falls, Pennsylvania, with Grandfather Carothers. I was on my first leave after graduation from Airborne School. At nineteen I was ready to face the world. Three young ladies spied my gleaming parachute boots, jump wings, and uniform. They ran up, and all three began to hug me. Each told me her name and asked if she could see me that evening.

A light turned on. Girls were interested in boys! How could I have lived so long and not understood that? From then on, when I saw an attractive girl, I no longer had to wrestle with fear. It was gone. The new and enlightened Merlin could walk up to anyone of the opposite sex and say the important opening words: "Hello, haven't I met you somewhere?" On hundreds of past occasions I could have said that, and there would have been no fear.

Think of it in this way: if we tried to walk on a two-by-four board as a bridge between two twenty-five-story buildings, most of us would be terrified. Why? Because we can't walk on a two-by-four board? It depends on where the board is. If we placed it on the ground, we wouldn't be afraid to walk on it. The same board, the same person, but no fear. Many of us seem to believe the "board" of which we are afraid spans a bottom-less chasm when in fact it rests firmly on the ground.

It is just as pointless to say, "I'm not afraid," if indeed you are, as it is to say, "I believe," if you don't. The objective is to be delivered from the power of fear and to clearly and honestly believe what you say you believe.

Freedom from fear begins with one step: to admit that we are afraid. Reasonable fear is an ally once we recognize it and place it in proper perspective. Our reluctance to admit fear can make us deny, fight, or try to control it. In so doing it controls us, even to the point of paralyzing or killing us.

Solo Flying

I'll never forget my first solo flight in an airplane. From my early teens I had dreamed that someday I would be a pilot, but it wasn't until I was twenty-nine that I fulfilled my dream. I actually owned half interest in the plane. That little Cessna had barely enough power to take off, but to me it was a mighty worker of miracles. It thrust me and my instructor up, up into the wild blue yonder. I was ecstatic. My dream was a reality.

Every flight was packed with excitement. Everything the instructor asked me to do gave me pure joy; heading back to the airport made me unhappy. I yearned to fly into space and orbit the world.

During every minute of my training flights, I looked forward to the moment when the instructor would say, "Today you will make your solo flight." That was the ultimate, the very summit of success—to fly all by myself! Each day I determined to handle my beautiful flying machine so expertly that the instructor would see I was ready.

The supreme moment of ecstasy finally arrived. I had

completed a successful landing when the instructor said, "Stop the plane, let me out, and take off on your own."

As I taxied down the runway I shouted, "This is it!"

Then, the glorious moment. At the end of the runway I was ready to go. With no tower on that little country airfield, the time of takeoff was up to me

After a few deep breaths I gripped the little throttle and carefully pushed it full forward. The "mighty" engine burst into action, and I began to taxi down the runway. In about two hundred feet, the plane began pulling to the left although the runway went straight ahead. I quickly turned the steering wheel to the right, but the plane kept going left. What was wrong?

Ahead I saw disaster in the making—six men digging a ditch on the left edge of the runway. My "gigantic" plane headed straight toward them. In panic I wrenched the wheel more to the right; the plane would not respond. With a seemingly obstinate determination the little propeller kept pulling me rapidly toward the workers who were paying no attention to my runaway craft.

My desperation mounted. The next few seconds seemed like forever. The whirling propeller could kill the workers. The frail craft could explode and ignite the gasoline. Seven lives were in peril!

The left wheel veered off the runway; the point of no return had arrived. Everything the instructor had said vanished from my mind, and fear took over. With the propeller a few yards from the workers, I managed a mighty heave on the controls. The plane lifted a few feet off the ground, missed the men and a fence by inches, and finally rose into the sky. I was safe, but my pride was shattered. Fear had destroyed my opportunity for a splendid performance.

With instructions to only circle the field and land, I dreaded facing the instructor. This student was a miserable failure.

"Well, Carothers, what did you do wrong?"

"Everything!"

"Do you know *exactly* what you did?" I knew. Dozens of times the instructor had said the steering wheel does not control the direction of an airplane on the ground.

"You turn a car with the steering wheel. You turn an airplane with rudders. Use your feet. Push the left rudder for left and the right rudder for right." In our dual takeoffs I had pushed the right rudder for a straight direction on the runway. When I was alone, fear had taken over, and everything I knew about controlling a plane on the ground flew out the window.

The instructor, instead of chewing me out, went over what I had done wrong and why, saying that panic was common on a first solo, and my reaction was not unusual. He had me take off a dozen more times with him. Finally he said, "Now you're on your own again." I made a perfect takeoff, and soon I became a licensed pilot. Since then I have flown for many hours and been in tight situations, but I never froze as I did on my first harrowing solo flight.

Flying helped me put fear into perspective. Instead of controlling me, fear became my ally. The guard dog of fear keeps me on my toes and reminds me of my limitations and, most of all, my need to depend on God. It persuades me to maintain my flying skills or stay out of the pilot's seat. But panic can turn fear into a snarling attacker, threatening to kill. When we take authority over it, and calmly say, "Down!" as with a charging dog, it frees our minds for the task ahead.

We can make an ally out of reasonable fear. In the following chapters we will examine some common roots of unreasonable fear, but first we will look at the source that conquers fear— our joyous faith!

CHAPTER 5

Faith to Climb Mountains

My wife, Mary, and I loaded our motor home for an impromptu visit to Yosemite National Park. What a magnificent sight it was!

There I learned a lesson that would bring important changes in my attitude about many things. It began on our second day there.

Five people stood near our campsite, peering up at Washington Tower. *What are they studying so intently?* I wondered. They passed a pair of binoculars from one to the other. Obviously something intrigued them.

As I studied the smooth, solid stone that seemed to jut straight up for twenty-five hundred feet, I could see nothing but rock. We were about three hundred yards from the base of the gigantic, awesome tower that reaches toward the sky. One of the group said, "Look, he's moving upward!" I looked, but there was no "he" in sight.

We had binoculars with us, so I decided to see what had captivated those folks. At first I saw nothing but the mountain. Then, about one thousand feet up the face of the tower, I saw what looked like a bright red dot. It was near two other spots, all linked by what seemed to be a rope.

I felt a knot in the pit of my stomach. Those spots were people on the smooth surface of solid rock. Were they crazy? Later I inquired around the campground to see if anyone knew what was going on.

"Oh, sure," said one man. "A different group of climbers goes up there every day."

"How far do they go?"

"All the way. Usually they make it partway in a day, spend the night on a ledge or hanging in a net, and then finish the next day."

"How many are killed?"

"Oh, they know what they're doing. They seldom even get hurt. Last year one man broke a leg, and a helicopter had to lift him off."

For a few days I was enchanted with watching groups of climbers. The knot in my stomach subsided a little as, through seven-power binoculars, I watched those tiny "spots" always get to the top by nightfall on their second day. But what kind of people would risk life and limb on such a hazardous sport? The mountain seemed all but impossible for humans to scale.

Mary and I made our way to its base, where the climb seemed even more formidable. The surface seemed nearly as smooth as a cement highway. *How could a person climb even twenty feet?* I wondered. To scale the entire mountain seemed impossible.

As we walked along we came upon a group of six men. Five of them were being trained in rock climbing. The sixth man had a rope that went through a pulley fastened about one hundred feet up. One end was attached to a trainee; the instructor held the other. As the student climbed a few feet up, the instructor pulled in the slack to keep him in a steady, safe grip.

We were enthralled. The student put his fingers in a nearly invisible perpendicular crack, then leaned to the right or left. His shoes appeared to be very thin, and the soles looked like coarse sandpaper. Attached to the back of his belt was a pouch with powder for his hands. The shoes seemed to cling to the smooth rock as though they had suction cups on them.

I realized that rock climbing is a skill that can be learned. My appetite for details was whetted, so I began to read about rock climbing to obtain more. However, I was looking for understanding, not participation.

One detail taught me a very important lesson about life. To ascend a precarious solid-stone mountain, a climber must learn to pace himself. This is the ability to get the most mileage, or altitude, from his available energy. If he uses up his reservoir of strength, exhaustion comes. If he climbs 2,400 feet up a 2,500-foot mountain and runs out of vitality, he may be stuck in the dark or in a storm. I would not want his problems! Making it to 2,400 feet isn't enough. He must make it to the top or to some safe spot en route.

Climbers use every conceivable way to conserve their energy. Prior to the trip, they eat foods for maximum nourishment. Food means weight, so they carefully select what they carry with them. Clothing at high altitudes and in chilling winds needs to be warm but light. Ropes and all equipment need to be of minimum weight but maximum strength. Expertise is required in the quantity and quality of the pack: sleeping bag, 150 feet of rope, hammer, webbing, carabiners, pitons, chock stones, wedges, nuts, angle irons, and clothing.

But most important, instructors insist, is the attitude of the climber. He must not be anxious or afraid. Why? The obvious reason is that fear inhibits the body's ability to function. A less obvious reason is the source of my important lesson.

Fear and anxiety use too much energy. Really? Yes! Serious climbers cannot afford the luxury of anxiety. Fear causes energy to evaporate.

People who would scale challenging mountains must first learn to be so confident in themselves that they thoroughly enjoy what they are doing. Instructors say, "Of course, everyone will eventually have anxious moments. But that has to be rare. Climbing must be exhilarating and fun, or the climber will be too exhausted to reach the top."

Most of us are never pitted against tasks that use maximum energy resources, so we seldom learn what causes us to lose energy. If we're too tired, we simply stop to rest or eat. Rock climbers often don't have those alternatives. Their lives and their success depend on reaching the top in the required time. If they run out of energy, they could make a fatal mistake—for themselves and those who depend on them.

Some Christians never persevere long enough to climb a spiritual mountain. If they fail to reach their goal quickly enough, they give up the task. Christians who are determined to reach certain goals need maximum spiritual energy. I have learned that this energy is quickly dissipated by fear. The Bible repeatedly cautions us against fear and anxiety. They cause our ability to reach spiritual goals to dissipate like energy seeping from a battery.

A battery-operated radio can pick up messages from a broadcasting station. But as the battery dies, the radio can no longer receive the signals.

This analogy is far from accurate, but it helps me to understand a vital factor in my spiritual life. If I allow myself to be anxious about *anything,* my spiritual battery gets weaker. Then when God has a message for me, my ability to receive His message is so weak that I can't hear what He is saying. The volume of His broadcast hasn't decreased in the slightest—only my ability to receive it.

If you wonder why you lack the spiritual energy to go out and tell others the good news of the gospel, perhaps fear has stolen your resources.

Picture Christians who have serious problems and have learned through years of practice to spend endless hours in worry. They wish they had made different decisions. They are afraid of the future. They cry out for direction from God, who speaks, but they can't hear Him. Their spiritual ability to hear is overwhelmed by their fears.

Would-be rock climbers could choose to stay on the ground, but you and I have no choice. We must be about the task of fulfilling our purpose here on earth.

We must daily surrender our self-proclaimed right to worry about our health, a job, the boss not liking us, our children, what our spouses might do, and so on. I have never heard a clear word from God or received a miracle for myself or another person unless I was abiding in His peace.

You may say, "That isn't fair. God should help me when I'm upset. That's when I need help the most." But regardless of our wishes, if we insist on our right to be anxious and fearful, we lose spiritual strength and cannot be victorious.

Yes, other people do not always understand why you are afraid. They haven't walked in your shoes. But for all of us the goal is still the same—to be free of fear.

The Bible says, "Don't be anxious" (Matt. 6:34 TLB). It's not that God doesn't like anxious people. He wants us to learn how to trust Him.

The army taught us how to make a parachute jump. The trainers told us to relax and not to worry. Not be worried? You gotta be kidding! The chute might not open! But they emphasized, "Don't be afraid when you leave the plane, and don't be afraid when you hit the ground."

Fortunately for me, the night before our first jump I went to sleep the minute my head hit the pillow. Other men lay awake all night. The next morning in the open airplane door they were tense, worried, and anxious. Some were so tired that they couldn't recall what we had been taught. Muscles were tight; they were primed for an accident. Instead of leaping boldly into the air as they were trained to do, they fell out and often became entangled in the dozens of lines of the parachute. Fear and lack of confidence in what they had been taught brought needless pain. And at times, fatal accidents!

An anxious paratrooper can be compared with the small branch of a tree that is dead. Consider how easy it is to snap a brittle, unbending twig, while a live branch will bend easily without breaking.

In nearly fifteen years of paratrooper training, I saw many men seriously injured because they had no faith in themselves or in their equipment. They left the plane with a tense knot of fear, and reaching the ground, they were still so tense, they broke legs and some even their spines. Not one of them wanted to get hurt. But they were controlled by their fears and had very little faith in their parachutes. That resulted in unnecessary suffering.

God says, "Don't be anxious. Don't be anxious at any time for any reason." A fearful paratrooper and a worried Christian seem to have some characteristics in common.

Consider our efforts to communicate with God and to ask His help with our problems. He knows that anxiety separates us from the help He wants to give. If we do not follow His instruction to trust Him, we approach prayer with a tense, anxious spirit. God seems far away. If our faith is weak, our efforts to trust God can easily crumble. We may never crash into the ground like a paratrooper, but anxiety and fear can delay the normal growth and maturity of our seed of faith.

I don't know why I could peacefully go to sleep the night before my first parachute jump. Or why some people can always pray with confidence and faith that God will hear and answer them.

I do know that some of my friends were injured seriously when they were anxious about jumping. I also know that anxiety is exactly the opposite of faith. Many prayers go unanswered when we are anxious.

Joy That Replaces Fear

When we know why our prayers are not being answered, we can concentrate on learning how to get rid of our fears and anxieties. Praise to God for everything can become a powerful ally.

The key is to release everything in our lives to God and believe He is working in and through everything for our good. We then receive and rejoice in the answer to our prayer before God does anything. We have peace in the knowledge that He has the right solution. If this seems too simple an explanation, please remember the paratrooper.

Picture the young man floating to the ground on his first jump. The last thing he wants is pain. Not one parachutist wants to be injured. Yet the one who is most afraid is the one most likely to be hurt.

The person most afraid that his prayers won't be answered is most likely to have little faith and, therefore, unanswered prayers.

Most of us have said to ourselves, "I believe! I believe!" when we really mean, "I *want* to believe, but my doubts are stronger than my believing."

I've learned a most helpful way to strengthen my faith. We know this Scripture is true: "We know that all that happens to us is working for our good if we love God and are fitting into his plans" (Rom. 8:28 TLB). Because this is true, we can know that God is in control of the details of our lives. When this truth is firmly settled in our hearts and minds, we find that it is not too difficult to give Him the thanks and praise that He desires in every situation in our lives (1 Thess. 5:18). As we do, we find—to our surprise—that praising and thanking God *for* our problems (as Eph. 5:20 tells us) actually cause our faith to grow and grow.

In turn our faith and confidence in God bring us joy: "Now when he had brought them into his house, he set food before them; and he rejoiced, having believed in God" (Acts 16:34); and "Though now you do not see Him, yet believing, you rejoice with joy inexpressible and full of glory" (1 Peter 1:8).

But Jesus cautioned us that the joy we have when we believe will leave us if we stop believing: "The ones on the rock are those who, when they hear, receive the word with joy; and these have no root, who believe for a while and in time of temptation fall away" (Luke 8:13).

As we say, "God, I believe You are answering my prayer in the way that will bring me the most good," we receive joy. This is a natural response to believing that God has all the details of life under His control. Jesus taught us to have faith like that of a little child. When a child believes she will receive the very best, what happens? Her face lights up! So, practice smiling when you say, "God, I believe You." Faith causes joy to increase, and that makes it fun to practice believing God.

I've learned a crucial lesson: fear and faith are reflected in our faces. Mark 9:20 tells us that the demon in a boy saw Jesus. That means demons can see us!

The Bible doesn't tell us that evil spirits can read our thoughts. But if they see joy in us, they must know it is the joy of the Lord. They then want to get away from us, just as they always wanted to get away from Jesus. Do you see how important it is for us to learn how to live in the incredible power of joy?

Even before Jesus came to earth, men prophesied that He would have "exultant joy and gladness above and beyond [His] companions" (Heb. 1:9 AMPLIFIED). The Greek word for gladness, *agalliasis*, means "much leaping." *The Living Bible* says Jesus had "more gladness . . . [than] anyone else" (Heb. 1:9).

Have you noticed that Jesus looked at people and saw they had faith to be healed? The Bible doesn't say He used His ability to read minds; He saw something in them. He must have seen the expectant joy in their faces as they believed He was going to heal them.

When we believe something good is about to happen, we react with joy. Joy and believing work so closely together that it is sometimes difficult to separate one from the other. Joy is a dynamo that can cause our faith to work. Even the demons must know this.

I believe this is why God has given us instructions in Philippians and Ephesians to rejoice always and to sing and make melody in our hearts. He knows that we are vulnerable to all kinds of torments if we aren't empowered with His joy.

God's joy in us is a little like gasoline is to a car engine. Joy equals power; joy causes us to get where we want to go.

Many cry, "Give me what I need (want), and then I'll shout with the voice of triumph." But the laws of faith work the same for you and me as they did for Abraham, Isaac, David, Peter, and Paul. When we believe, we receive. Joy is the fuel that creates the power of our faith. Little joy results in

- little strength.
- unfulfilled desires.
- no overflowing of hope.

According to 2 Corinthians 3:18, we reflect the glory of the Lord. The word used for glory means "dazzling" or "glittering." I strongly recommend that all of us learn to have that glory working in us.

If you walk into a dark room, you might stub your toes, bang your head, or even fall flat on your face. But find a tiny light switch, turn it on, and enjoy light flowing from a distant power plant. As long as the switch stays on, the power keeps flowing.

God's unlimited joy will flow into our lives if we keep the switch of praise turned on. Absence of joy causes us to stumble in the darkness of life's problems. We can't create joy, any more than a light switch creates light. But we are able to turn on God's joy by giving Him the continual sacrifice of praise (Heb. 13:15). I bumbled along for many years in a gloom. There was confusion regarding my physical problems; I faced deaths in my family, and I had anxieties about the future. The horrors I had experienced during several wars haunted my dreams. *Until* I learned to praise and thank God for everything in my life.

If darkness seems to surround you, don't give up. This book can be just what you need to throw on God's magnificent light switch.

Corrie ten Boom wrote about her experiences as a captive in a German concentration camp during World War II. She and her sister, Betsy, were in the worst prison camp and in a flea-infested barracks. What darkness! Betsy told Corrie they needed to thank God for each detail, including the fleas. At first Corrie refused to praise the Lord for the horrible little insects, but then she united with Betsy. During their months at the camp they were able to freely hold prayer and Bible study meetings without the guards intruding. The reason? The guards would not enter that barracks because of the fleas. As a direct result of her concentration camp experiences, Corrie went on to win thousands of people to Christ.

In William Law's eighteenth-century classic, *A Serious Call to a Devout and Holy Life,* he wrote,

> Would you know who is the greatest saint in the world? It is not he who prays most or fasts most; it is not he who gives most alms, or is most eminent for temperance, chastity, or justice, but it is he who is always thankful to God, who wills everything that God willeth, who receives everything as an instance of God's goodness, and has a heart always ready to praise God for it.

Believing that God causes everything to work for our good turns our joy switch on. He wants to help us believe but doesn't want to help too much. If we see too much evidence that He is working, we may then look for evidence rather than learn to believe without evidence. In the next chapter we'll see a few occasions in which God gave evidence, but only enough to encourage me onward.

CHAPTER 6

Yes, but What If?

My wife, Mary, and I visited Expo '86 in Vancouver. We did not expect the incredible things that happened when an "angel" took a special interest in our trip.

Everything we heard about Expo was good, except for the lo-o-o-ng lines for the best programs and hours of waiting. Friends urged us to take folding chairs. It's worth it, they encouraged, but be prepared for aching feet. One young man told us that his feet had gone from numbness to a feeling of being stomped on by ten overweight elephants.

To me, standing that long was aching, throbbing agony. I had suffered miles of lines—twenty years of them—in military service. My feet had long since been brutalized by frostbite, forced marches, and backbreaking loads, and they were vulnerable. My instant reaction to lines was fear bordering on panic. My fear said, "Stay away from Expo '86!" But I had learned new lessons about fear; it can rob us of confidence and happy experiences.

What does going to a world's fair have to do with overcoming fear? I felt I should disregard my old fears and go to Vancouver as if I expected it to be a painless delight. With great determination I told myself, "Merlin, you will not be afraid of long lines."

I wrote for a booklet on bed-and-breakfast accommodations in Vancouver. We had enjoyed staying in private homes in England and thought it would be interesting to do so in Canada. We selected one and took a taxi there. The family was delightful, telling us many things about Expo and how long the lines would be!

The next morning we had a fabulous breakfast in the dining room and then took a forty-five-minute bus ride through the city. It was a sunny Friday in September, and we had folding chairs and books to read to cope with the tedious lines.

Praying for supernatural help had never occurred to us, secure in our confidence that God works everything for our good. We were prepared to endure.

At the entrance, people moved in every direction. Millions of people, it seemed. We hadn't the faintest idea of where to go or how to get there. Lines seemed to reach for miles to all points of the compass, and we couldn't see where they started or ended.

All we could think of was, *Thank You, Lord*. Then the thought came: *What good will come of all this?* I knew of the marvelous Christian Pavilion at Expo, so I thought, *Perhaps You have all these people here for an opportunity to hear the good news*.

My heart was at peace. Without striving to accept the situation or asking God to intervene, I was enjoying the moment. For sure, I hadn't reacted that way during my twenty years in the army. There I'd learned to be an expert complainer, but I knew now that the thousands of hours of standing in lines were in preparation for what God wanted to teach me.

The main line in front of us seemed to be one hundred miles long, and it wove back and forth at the British Columbia Pavilion. *Great,* I thought, *here is a place we have been urged to see*. We asked an employee: "What do we do?"

"Have you tickets for this pavilion?"

"No, where do we get in line?"

"Come back tomorrow morning at eight, and get in the line marked 'Tickets.'"

"How long will it take to get them?"

"Probably an hour or more, but don't be late or you won't get tickets. Your tickets will be stamped with the hour you can see the program. Get into the pavilion line about two hours before it begins or you may lose out."

Our heads spun a bit, but however long it took, we were ready for the grand event.

Suddenly a man appeared and asked us if we would like two tickets. I expected to pay, thinking scalpers hadn't taken long to find us. Were they good ones, or were they counterfeits?

He handed them over, asked for nothing in return, then left.

The tickets were stamped for 10:50 A.M. Hey! That's the next program! We moved toward the pavilion sign that read 10:50 A.M. PROGRAM and soon found ourselves at the head of the line. I expected the attendant to say, "I don't know how you got these tickets, but they are counterfeit," and to call the police. But in minutes we were in the theater for the film we'd heard so much about. We had been at Expo less than twenty minutes.

I've tried many times to understand why the man gave us the tickets. Who was he? Why did he disappear so quickly? The odds against anyone standing in line for hours to get tickets and then giving them to me are at least a million to one. I believe our benefactor was sent by God.

The film of British Columbia's panoramic scenes was incredible.

It was lunchtime. We were warned that food lines also were very long. At the nearby Saskatchewan Restaurant we saw about one hundred people in line. Since the Lord had already been so good to us, we were not too disappointed. But then we decided to look for the restaurant that was located in the Ontario Pavilion instead. We took about fifty steps and there it was, right in front of us.

Its walkway was an upward winding one about two hundred feet long, with no one in line. *It must be closed,* we thought.

But in moments we were shown to the last empty table, with a picture-window view of the fabulous inlet, False Creek. Ferries and cruise and pleasure boats bobbed under a gorgeous Canada sun. The meal was superb—close to perfect. When the Lord wants to especially bless us, He knows how. He doesn't always provide exquisite meals for Mary and me; far from it. But at that special time He arranged to teach us important lessons.

I had a warm glow in my heart. I knew God had intervened in our affairs, saying, "Merlin, I can do anything any time, to meet any need you have. Don't ever be afraid."

I heard a couple at the next table speak of a marvelous three-dimensional film they had seen there in the Ontario Pavilion. It was a must-see, they said, echoing others. They had come to Expo an hour before it opened, and then waited in line three hours for the film *Discovery.* "Fantastic," they said.

"Is it worth standing in line for three hours?" I asked.

"By all means! It's the most unusual film we have ever seen. Stand in line, however long it takes!"

Following their directions, we arrived at the Discovery Theater, with only a few people around it. We just knew it couldn't be the right place. Hundreds of people would be in line. Mary asked an attendant if it was the place to line up. He said, "Yes, but this isn't the main entrance, and if you go into the theater this way, you can't see the preliminary exhibits."

Those exhibits, we had been told, were the only part not worth standing in line for.

Ten minutes after our fabulous lunch we were in line for the film; then another extraordinary thing happened. Almost immediately the door opened, and we were shown to the best seats. Other people had waited three hours, but we were inside in less than two minutes.

The three-dimensional film was indeed a discovery. Unforgettable. It had breathtaking qualities. Pictures seemed to leave the screen and move up to our faces. Geese in formation turned and seemed to fly right at us; a woman in front of us ducked her head. Did God love Mary and me more than the others? No. He chose that day to show us He could do anything, any time, anyplace. Our only obligation was to trust Him. If He knew I needed to stand in many lines over the course of many years, His love could arrange it, but only as a blessing. From those countless times of waiting in army lines, I learned that it was special training for those of us who tend to be impatient.

The hours the Lord saved us from waiting in lines at Expo enabled us to have just enough time to visit the Pavilion of Promise. After a movie and live presentation, we were invited into a chapel, given a pamphlet with a gospel message, and led in a prayer of repentance. Each person was asked to raise a hand if he or she wanted to accept Jesus as Savior. The man in charge told us that every day hundreds of people raised their hands.

Those experiences reinforced my growing conviction that God wants to help us renounce any fears that might defeat His objectives. Soon I would have another lesson in the power of faith that overcomes fear.

Midnight Calls

The piercing ring of the telephone forced my eyes open. The clock showed midnight.

"Merlin, I'm in a telephone booth in the middle of nowhere, and I can't find Genie. Have you heard from her?"

Telephone booth? Our daughter missing? What was Mary talking about? Why isn't Mary here? I struggled to come awake. I then recalled that she had left several hours earlier to be with our daughter while Genie delivered her third child.

Before Mary got there, our daughter-in-law, Shelly, had called the doctor. He was some forty miles away, and the delivery was scheduled to be in his office. The baby was due and saying, "I'm coming!" Genie had to get to the doctor's office immediately. They made a dash in that direction.

When Mary arrived at the doctor's office, his doors were locked and the windows dark.

I was wide awake. Fear made a bold attack on my heart. Where was our daughter? Was she in an accident? Where was Mary? From what dark, lonely phone booth had she called? I had failed to ask her. What should I do?

For a long while I wrestled with my fears, then realized that if it is true that I can trust God, then I need not have fearful thoughts. I must remember how perfectly God works all things for our good.

Our daughter Genie did not make it to the doctor's office until after the birth. No accident, just the normal workings of nature. While Shelly was racing to get her there, Genie said, "It's too late; the baby's coming!"

"Coming! It can't come now. We are in the middle of nowhere."

"Sorry, but it's coming."

Our frantic daughter-in-law stopped at a gas station and asked for the nearest hospital.

"There's a little one up the road a piece."

Up the road a piece! They raced to the emergency entrance. "Help! Quick! A baby's coming."

"We have no facilities here for babies."

"But she's delivering now, in the car!" A startled doctor ran out. Genie was in the backseat of the car, taking pictures of the baby.

"Doctor, is it a boy or a girl?"

"If you would stop flashing the camera, I could see!"

Daughter and granddaughter were both well. There had been no need to be afraid. Genie said later that while on the wild car ride, she kept saying, "Thank You, Lord. I know You will use this for my good." And He did.

Fear of Sickness

My physical infirmities have often tempted me to have fearful thoughts. Each illness required me to accept one of two alternatives:

1. I'm sick and getting sicker.
2. I'm sick, but God is healing me.

The first was no option at all; I felt continually depressed.

As we grow older, negative thoughts become increasingly easier to adopt: *If I'm hurting now, I'll surely hurt more when I'm a few years older. What will happen to me when I get too ill to take care of myself? What happens when my money runs out and I can't work?* Such thoughts could make every day miserable. Many older people are haunted by such speculations. So, readers of every age, please listen and heed.

Thoughts based on fear breed more of the same.

Thoughts based on faith in God result in peace and joy.

There was a time when a bad night's sleep would set me up for a bad day. It would begin with the thought: *Today will be rough. Loss of sleep will make me tired all day.* My day was controlled by my negative thoughts. Eventually I realized the foolishness of my attitude. Instead of expecting a bad day I began to expect a good one. Lack of sleep could work for me instead of against me. To my joy, I've found that expecting the best consistently helps me to enjoy days that otherwise would be unpleasant.

My ninety parachute landings had exacerbated the arthritis in my spine. Such an ailment is a marvelous aid to self-pity and self-protection. I practiced worrying about how much weight I could lift without injuring my poor spine. I would warily pick up a twenty-five-pound item and wonder if it would be too much of a strain. What a burden! What fear!

If you haven't suffered from spinal problems, you may not know how excruciatingly painful they can be. It is easy to live in fear that the pain might develop into endless misery. But I've learned that I can joyfully believe that God is healing me.

You may have a totally different problem, but the solution is the same. Practice believing that God is healing your body or is solving your problems. Your faith will grow, and you will gradually—perhaps even rapidly—realize that He is creating a fresh new attitude in you: "God who gives you hope will keep you happy and full of peace as you believe in him. I pray that God will help you overflow with hope in him" (Rom. 15:13 TLB).

Let me share another personal experience. As an army soldier, I was continually with men who took great pride in their physique. Unfortunately that attitude became part of my thought pattern without my even wanting to think that way. Part of me knew that physical strength had nothing to do with learning to trust God to supply our needs, but another part of me was proud of my excellent health.

As I grew older, it became crystal clear that my physical strength was declining. That did not mean that God loved me any less; it meant Merlin was getting older. But I didn't like that, and sometimes I grumbled.

Recently I was doing the exercises I try to do every day. As I frequently did, I was bemoaning the fact that as the years go by, I can do less and less. Then I received an inner revelation: "Merlin, what you are thinking is not right. The reason you are losing your physical strength is that you are getting closer to the time when you will go to heaven!"

My attitude changed. I began to rejoice in the exercises that I can still do. For the first time in months, I was able to thoroughly enjoy the strength that God gives me.

Then I thought of something else. When I die, I will not be able to move any part of my body. No big revelation, I know. But when that happens to my body, I will actually be in heaven!

God may not give us perfect health, even though we might think He should. But flawless health is not necessarily a measure of our faith. Faith helps us to accept our present state of health and to glory in our confidence that God always wants to work good in and for us. Even getting old can be a blessing! My time of exercising has become more enjoyable to me than it was when I was young and full of vigor.

If we believe God is *not* working for our good, the body cooperates and says, "I agree! I feel terrible." The truth is, if God stopped all of the healing and restoration that is continually working in our bodies, we would soon die. A small cut in the skin could cause death. If God withdrew our capacity to sleep, we would soon be asleep in the grave.

If you break an arm, you would be wise to visit a physician, who would x-ray the bone and set it. Then you can go on your way believing your arm is healing.

But some infirmities are very different. The doctor may not know what to do, and we might feel helpless. We then have the opportunity to believe that God heals us by His power.

James 1:6–8 tells us, "Let him ask in faith, with no doubting, for he who doubts is like a wave of the sea driven and tossed by the wind. For let not that man suppose that he will receive anything from the Lord; he is a double-minded man, unstable in all his ways."

What most often causes us to doubt? Not seeing results.

During the Persian Gulf War, at a meeting in San Antonio I prayed with an army officer and his wife. He was discouraged and looked quite miserable. His back had been severely injured, and he was permanently off flying status. To a pilot, that is like telling him he has an incurable disease. His wife had a far worse problem. She had a cancerous growth in her breast and a tumor in the abdomen. As I prayed for them, there was no outward evidence of an immediate healing.

The next day the pilot reported to his army doctor and asked to be reexamined. Doctors regularly get this request from men who have been taken off flying status. This one told the pilot, "I'm sorry, but you will never again be able to fly for the army." The man persisted; the doctor gave in and had X rays taken of the "permanently" fused disks. The results confused the doctor but elated the officer. Nothing was wrong with his spine!

At home he told his wife, "We must get you back to your doctor. You may be healed also." She had another mammogram and an X ray of her abdomen. All cancers were gone! Sometime later Mary and I met the couple during a series of meetings in San Antonio. At each service the beaming couple told everyone, "We are healed!"

When Mary and I pray for others, we always like to see immediate results, but God has taught us to pray and to leave the healing in His hands. Time after time people call or write us: "When you prayed, we felt nothing, but every day we keep feeling a little better." Often they have had serious infirmities for many years. After seeing this happen so often, Mary and I know that God honors prayers if we pray, believe, and keep on believing.

Too often Christians try to believe one way while feeling another way. Have you seen the dour-faced expression of one who says, "I have all kinds of faith, but nothing good happens"? It would be more correct for that person to say, "I do not believe God will answer my prayer; therefore, I feel miserable."

Many Christians develop a theological confession such as, "I'm supposed to believe that God is doing something for me; therefore, I believe He is." But a theological statement is not faith. When we believe, we have corresponding joy.

Once we realize how crucial it is that we believe what we say, then we will concentrate on learning to believe. We can learn. Our task may seem difficult, but it need not be. We can approach our goals with anticipation and gladness. We are working with the Holy Spirit to become more like Christ.

In the next chapter let's learn more about how to increase our faith.

CHAPTER 7

Learn and Believe

Believing requires learning. We can learn, one step at a time, to discard a lifetime habit of believing only what we see or feel. A moment of reflection will convince us that what we see and what we feel are often the complete opposites of what is true.

Consider the room or place in which you read this book. Is it still, or is it moving? Is the earth moving or still? The truth is that the place in which you sit whirls through space at thousands of miles per hour. What you feel or see is often very unreliable.

When you use your faith, you do not rely on what you see or feel. You say, "God, Jesus promised that if I believe, You would work healing in me." You can't see or feel the healing of a broken arm, but you can believe that it is happening.

God may heal you through doctors, or He may lead you to change your diet or perhaps to exercise more. There are various pathways to health. God may even work a miracle. But expect the miracle that *He* selects. Naaman expected a dramatic miracle, but when Elisha told him to wash in the Jordan River seven times, he was disgusted and thought Elisha was a fraud. When Naaman finally heeded Elisha's advice, he was healed (2 Kings 5:14).

You and I should accept God's healing through whatever means He selects. Our part is to believe and to keep on believing. Jesus made a simple promise to us: "All things are possible to him who believes" (Mark 9:23).

Jesus' faith always produced instant miracles. Perhaps because of this, we Christians want our faith to work instantly, and some even demand that it do so. If it doesn't, they give up. But often, faith works gradually.

At a meeting in Maryland I prayed for a boy of ten. There were no obvious results. Neither the parents nor I could see any evidence of a miracle. Then, this letter came to me the next month:

> You prayed for our son Christopher at your meeting last month in Bel Air, Maryland. He was epileptic and mentally retarded. Just two days after that meeting, Chris brought home a note congratulating us on his improvement. After a year and a half at that special school, this was the first encouraging note we had received!
>
> Now, for the first time in his ten years, Chris can go up and down stairs! He is happier and better in every way.

Jesus was perfect, yet even He had to learn in order to mature. As a young boy, "Jesus increased in wisdom and stature, and in favor with God and men" (Luke 2:52).

When we have severe pain, we normally want the quick relief offered by the shot of medication that a doctor gives. But quick solutions that are misused can eventually cause other problems such as drug addiction. In most situations we need to seek more permanent solutions. Jesus gave us His solution when He said, "If you can believe, all things are possible to him who believes" (Mark 9:23). I'm convinced that He intended this statement to encourage us. We can grow in faith until our faith helps us solve any problem!

What if we have no known illness, but for some unknown reason we feel miserable? Most of us have days like that. Faith gives us the power to overcome our feelings.

Angels do not always appear. Prison doors do not always spring open. But believing always changes people. I have known hundreds of people who lived in nightmares of suffering but were transformed into creatures of joy when they turned their fears into faith.

If you suffer from some infirmity, I encourage you to tell God, "I believe You are healing me." Continue to believe that He is. Don't look at the outward circumstances. If you don't feel better tomorrow, don't look upon that as failure. The body often feels extra sick when it is being mended.

Our feelings nearly always want to overpower our faith in God's promises. But sometimes there are hidden clues in the way we feel. If you pray for something good and believe you receive it, how do you feel? You feel happy! That is part of the reaction we always have when we expect something good. We feel unhappy when we *don't* believe that God is answering our prayers.

If you are convinced that your employer will never give you a raise, no matter how hard you work or how excellent your performance, how do you feel when you think about a raise? You don't believe you are going to get it, and you don't feel good about that.

If there is a possibility that your boss will raise your pay, but you only hope for it, do you feel good about it? A little nebulous, isn't it? Sometimes you expect it and you feel good, but at other times you expect to never get higher pay and you feel bad.

If your employer says in writing, "Your work has been superior, and as of today you have a 25 percent raise," you feel great, even though you still do not have any extra dollars in your hands. Your believing and your feelings are in agreement.

Tell children that you will give them something they want, and see the expressions on their faces. They will express exactly what they believe will happen.

When you and I tell God we believe He will answer our prayers, doesn't He see the expressions on our faces? More than that, doesn't He know exactly what is in our hearts?

For much of my life I've been afraid to unite faith and feelings. I tried carefully to avoid any thought of how I happened to feel when I was trying to bolster my faith. Then one day I received a marvelous insight that revolutionized my prayers.

Feelings should not control faith, but I had not learned the other part of this truth: faith should control feelings. As I learned to practice this principle, many of my old feelings were changed. It definitely wasn't easy. Old habits die hard.

Whenever my feelings controlled my faith, I noticed that I became discouraged. But the potential for change was so intriguing that I persevered. I learned that when I prayed for joy and peace, I needed to practice my faith by believing that God was indeed working good in me. As Jesus said, "These things I have spoken to you, that My joy may remain in you, and that your joy may be full" (John 15:11). Later He added, "These things I speak in the world, that they may have My joy fulfilled in themselves" (John 17:13). As I began to believe that God was working good in me, my feelings followed my faith. That inspired me!

The same principle works when we pray for health. As we believe God is healing us, our feelings should say, "That's right! I am getting better!"

If we say, "I am discouraged because of this and this and this," we are mistaken. We are discouraged because our feelings are controlling our faith. Doubt brings discouragement and fear. Expectation brings delight.

If you have a miserable job, it will be even more so next month unless something changes. Chances are slim that the people you work with, or for, will change. But you can change. Practice dozens of times each day declaring that God is helping you to enjoy your work. Don't just say, "God, You are helping me to enjoy my work." Believe that He is.

"But my job is too horrible for anyone to enjoy," you may say. If Paul and Silas could enjoy heavy chains in prison, surely God is able to help us learn to enjoy our work. Many people will say that Paul did not enjoy his time in prison, for to them that would be ridiculous or impossible. But Paul said he had learned how to find joy in his troubles. If you find this difficult to understand, I encourage you to read my book *Power in Praise*. It explains Paul's amazing discoveries regarding all things working for his good.

I do not suggest that you try to force yourself to enjoy your daily tasks. That would be akin to pulling yourself up by your bootstraps. Faith is different. It cooperates with God. It is believing that He is helping you to enjoy your employment and your life just as they are.

Jesus believed He was victorious when He was arrested and beaten. He claimed victory even when He was dying. Why was His belief so strong? He knew He would be resurrected. Death was absolutely necessary to His resurrection.

You and I can be victorious when faced with infirmities, problems, or suffering. Why? Because we, too, will be resurrected! And *everything we experience* prepares us for this.

They mocked and challenged Jesus to come down from the

cross if He was God. We will hear similar challenges echoing in our minds: *If God is helping me, why doesn't He . . . ?* But like Jesus, we can see by faith the joy that is set before us. Forever and ever we will rejoice with Him in our eternal victory.

Confess to God, "Today You are healing my body, my business, my marriage, or my problems. Your joy is filling my heart."

In Hebrews 11, God especially honors people who trusted Him. For dozens of years they patiently waited for answers to their prayers. Faith that works often needs to be practiced hundreds of times a day. *God is healing me.* This faith works for the man or woman who has a simple cold or for the person who is seriously ill.

The body can quickly heal a slight cut without assistance. A larger wound requires a bandage, antibiotics, and much care. The body can heal a simple cold, but a serious illness may need medical aid *and* faith.

Faith helps us get well; God designed us that way.

A child of nine months finds it difficult to walk and needs encouragement to keep trying. He must try hundreds of times. Eventually he will run. Can he run a mile in four minutes? That takes more years of sometimes painful discipline.

Faith, too, requires discipline: "God, You are taking care of this problem. I rejoice! I'm glad! I trust You! I will not hang my head in fear or worry! You are using this problem in some way to bless me! I am victorious!"

Jesus said to Martha, "Martha, Martha, you are worried and troubled about many things" (Luke 10:41). Some Christians are troubled about many things. But Philippians 4:4 says, "Rejoice in the Lord always." "Always" means every minute. That's God's plan. It's the kind of faith that works healing and brings joy and happiness to those who choose trust in God instead of fear. Our objective is to be delivered from fears and to believe what we say we believe.

Consider the woman who came to Jesus with "a flow of blood" that caused her to suffer for twelve years (Mark 5:25). Many doctors treated her, but she became worse, spent all her money, and had every reason to feel defeated. But she refused to give up. She heard about Jesus, and "she said, 'If only I may touch His clothes, I shall be made well'" (Mark 5:28). When she touched His clothing, she was made well. Why?

Before we answer, we should first hear Jesus' response to her. He said, "Your faith has made you well" (Mark 5:34). But her own thoughts caused her to believe. She thought the right thoughts. My message throughout this book is simple: what you think is important!

Remember, the woman didn't even ask Jesus for help. She believed that if she touched Him, she would be well. The moment she combined believing and touching Him, the miracle happened.

It wasn't the touching that healed her. A thousand people might have touched Jesus' garments that day, for He was surrounded by people who were struggling to get near Him. Only this woman was healed. If we could touch Jesus' body today, we would receive nothing unless we also believed.

Many prayers for healing are lazy and unwise—like the farmer who asks God to sow his seeds. He wants good crops but without toil.

We received this letter: "When you were in Cincinnati in April 1991, you prayed for my daughter. She is eleven, and has battled scoliosis, and a crooked back, for many years. She lived with continual pain. She had an immediate change—the pain decreased. Within two days her back was straight and she had no pain!"

My wife and I have had the joy of praying for thousands of people. The results? Some said they felt no improvement in health or happiness. Some reported instant healing. But most said a process began that caused their health and happiness to improve in ways that amazed them.

Do your best to be unaffected by symptoms or by how long you have felt this way or that. Be well in your spirit. Let Jesus' Spirit be yours. Let Him select the best way to honor your faith. Do this, and fear will disappear.

Now let's consider what fear might do to us and the marvelous changes that faith brings.

CHAPTER 8

Fear of Death

"You ou nearly scared me to death!" What was the source of this strange expression? Where did the idea arise that one could be frightened to death? Is fear really *that* powerful? Throughout history there have been reports of fear causing persons to die.

A French author, writing on the French Revolutionary period, told of such an incident. A prisoner was forced to extend his arm through a small opening in a wall. On the other side, his captors bound his hand and told him that blood was dripping into a pan from a cut in his finger. They pricked his finger with a pin and dripped warm water over it and into a pan.

They kept telling the prisoner how much "blood" he was losing. One captor said, "He has lost a quart! His heartbeat is slowing!"

The captors pretended to discuss his vital signs and loudly described an increasingly weakened condition as the warm water dripped. The author of the account said the prisoner's heart began to respond to his fear. He had a heart attack and died.

Fear can cause heart attacks. In military operations I have seen men so paralyzed with fear that muscles in their bodies would not move. Heart muscles could easily do the same. I have seen men prepare for combat with no apparent fear. They felt invincible. But many of the same men had a different attitude when they became seriously wounded. The possibility of life after death was for them of paramount interest.

Life is a paradox. It seems to demand that we cleave to it while it preordains eventual surrender to eternity.

Seeing Life After Death

For many years I believed that to leave this earth and enter heaven would be glorious, but who wants to hurry it along? I felt a dread for the unknown that lay ahead—until one eventful night. I looked through a window that opened into forever.

After many years with uneventful nights of sleep, I had a strange experience that changed my attitude toward life, death, and eternity. It all began suddenly one night when I felt suspended in midair near the ceiling in our bedroom. I looked down to see myself lying in bed. *This is strange,* I thought. *No, it's impossible. No one will ever believe this!*

Never had I encountered anything that even remotely compared with the event. It is hard to explain how I can be certain that some part of me was fully awake while my body was asleep.

Paul expressed a similar sense of confusion when he said, "Whether in the body I do not know, or whether out of the body I do not know, God knows" (2 Cor. 12:2).

The wide-awake Merlin Carothers was about twelve feet away from the "me" I saw on the bed. The thought came: *How did I get up here?*

I seemed to be suspended above and to the left of a beautiful, ever-changing scene that appeared to be about fifty feet away. As I looked, I saw a brilliant, flowing river, all the colors of the rainbow, plus what seemed to be an infinity of hues. Even more spectacular was the water itself. It was alive!

How to describe "living" water? It appeared to move within itself, revolving, sparkling, bubbling, dancing, almost seeming to laugh. I wanted to watch that water forever.

Grass on the bank appeared green, yet it, too, seemed to embody every color. Green one minute, then multicolored as it moved. We normally think of green grass as alive. But that grass was so much more alive. It seemed to move about in happy, effortless waves. Rows of multihued flowers were reminiscent of an orchestra, harmonious, flowing in rhythm.

Nearby were elegant, graceful trees that appeared to preside over the flawless panorama. They were "speaking," but I could not understand. Strength seemed to flow from them. Their fruit resembled nothing I had ever seen. The scene radiated joy and peace. I wanted to enter it and stay forever.

As I strove to move closer to the incredible scene, a power held me in a firm but gentle grasp. The more I struggled, the more firmly I was held back.

Not yet, Merlin, came a voice of authority and strength. I knew I should not resist it, and I was slowly pulled away. It was unbearable to think of leaving; then I awoke, and it was daylight.

I have known people who waged gallant battles to stay alive until just a few minutes before death. They saw something so beautiful, they wanted to reach out to claim it. But those persons were gone so quickly that I could not learn what they saw.

Back to Earth

I walked to the window as I did every morning. The hills and lush green valley around our home were as beautiful as ever. But that morning something seemed wrong. Our beautiful hills and valley looked dead. The scene no longer held any magic for me. What had changed? Only my perspective.

That entire day I was in a daze. I knew I had experienced something that was changing me. In contrast to my vision, the world around me seemed faded and worn. My attitude toward death was changed. I knew that someday I would plunge into that same living water I had seen. Oh, Death, what joy you will bring!

I looked up Bible references. I had never questioned the meaning of the living water Jesus described to John in Revelation 7:17: "The Lamb . . . [will] lead them to living fountains of waters. And God will wipe away every tear from their eyes."

I don't know how to interpret all I saw, but I understand that life after death will introduce us immediately to the real, living world. What we see here on our planet is damaged and polluted. Every animal and plant struggles to stay alive. Everything is in the process of dying. But our next world is eternal. God's plan is breathtaking. One tiny glimpse filled my heart with expectation. I can't tell you why He gave me that glimpse. Perhaps it was for you.

You may be wrestling with problems and thinking, *Will they never end?* Oh, yes. They are in the process of fading away and dying. But in eternity, everything is designed to increase in beauty and strength and purity. How can perfection increase in perfection? I don't know, but I will enjoy learning.

The vision I saw enlarged my understanding of the lack of importance of this present world. Everything we see and touch is passing away. Even Satan will one day be gone. Until then, when difficulties confront you, remember that Satan wants you to think that things are bad and getting worse. The truth is that things are bad and getting worse for him.

When Jesus was here, He evaluated everything as to its true worth. He compared one hundred years of life on earth with eternity as a mere blink of an eye. I am growing in understanding this. My vision of the living water, grass, flowers, and trees was a mere sip at the fountain of living water. All of that will serve only as background to the dazzling, magnificent presence of God.

I wondered if the vision would lead to new understanding. It came some months later.

I was asleep, but barely. My restless slumber was broken by a severe pain along my spine. As I turned from side to side in those predawn hours, I wrestled with my persistent problem: *Why do I hurt so much? Why doesn't God heal me as He has done at other times? For how long can this pain intensify? Have my days of usefulness ended?*

Then I heard an inner voice, *You aren't filled with joy, Merlin.*

"No, Lord, I am not. I can't be. I hurt too much."

Yes, you can.

So I began to say, "Thank You, Lord, for this pain." After a few minutes of praising Him, the pain was the same, but I felt a glimmer of hope. I praised Him for the gift of eternal life and the joy of knowing Jesus as Savior.

The sun had not yet lightened the day, but a new joy blazed in my heart. Just before daybreak, I opened my Bible to Revelation 22:1. I had quoted it often: "And he showed me a pure river of water of life."

I realized the extraordinary blessing God had given me. But I would not have received that realization if I had not praised my way from discouragement to joy in my battle with pain. Thousands of times I had felt sorry for myself without realizing that my self-pity did nothing to help me receive something good.

Now I believe the Lord helped me so I could help you when you face your own hours of pain. Don't be discouraged, ever!

Receiving Good Things

I've often failed to receive good things because I misinterpreted Isaiah 40:31: "Those who wait on the LORD shall renew their strength." To me, waiting meant having patience until God came and did something for me. As He renewed my strength, it became clear what waiting means. It is in the same sense that a waiter serves in a restaurant. He doesn't sit around until the customer pays him. No, he serves him. Waiting on God means serving Him. When I actively praised God for His blessings to me, I served Him. That prepared the way for Him to renew my strength. But my service had to be done in joy. It's rather difficult to convince God that I'm joyful if I'm not.

If you are experiencing difficulties, I urge you to find opportunities to serve, to wait on God. You don't need to quit your job and become a paid, full-time minister. Serve Him by doing what you can to help the people around you. Serve your spouse, your neighbors, or the people with or for whom you work. Remember two significant details:

1. "Inasmuch as you did it to one of the least of these . . . you did it to Me" (Matt. 25:40).
2. "Serve the LORD with gladness" (Ps. 100:2).

For then you shall "obtain joy and gladness, and sorrow and sighing [complaining] shall flee away" (Isa. 35:10).

A martyr's attitude accomplishes little or nothing. Service needs to come from a joyful heart.

If we just endure our painful situations, we may feel spiritual, but God wants to use them to help us grow spiritually.

Self-pity is as dangerous to spiritual maturity as poison is to the body.

Most of us have had considerable practice at thinking, *Why did this have to happen to me?* The fallen part of our nature seems inclined to concentrate on our problems. It is susceptible to thinking about things that are painful and fearful.

God made us capable of thinking about good and lovely things. We must learn to *choose* to think His thoughts rather than anxious, fearful thoughts.

Have you ever awakened in the morning thinking, *Oh, no, it's time to get up?* It's easy to entertain such unhappy thoughts. You may feel that your life couldn't be worse. You have needs in every area; nothing is getting better. The fallen nature loves to moan about everything. The older you get, the more automatic your negativity becomes. But God has a better way.

Philippians 4:19 declares, "My God shall supply all your need according to His riches in glory by Christ Jesus." Many people place a negative twist on this verse, with emphasis on the "shall supply." They think that as long as God has not yet supplied their needs, they still have a right to be unhappy. That verse was written nearly two thousand years ago and has been in force ever since. God does supply our needs now. Right now is the moment in which we are to rejoice. We have exactly what we need. Until we learn that, we cannot receive the blessings from God that we desire, and fear is always there to push its way into every situation.

Tomorrow, next week, or a month from now, you may feel distressed. When that occurs, remember what you have learned. God's desire is that you enter His promised land. He created you with the physical, emotional, and spiritual need to live in peace. Ask any physician. Unhappiness causes stress in every organ of the body. When unhappiness becomes severe enough, the body can react with sickness or even death.

Jesus told us that God offers us a new opportunity to be unencumbered with the disease of unhappiness.

Grumbling

God told the Israelites to stop grumbling, complaining, and being unhappy. They refused. As an object lesson to all future generations, He caused two to three million of them to die in the desert. Only two men of that generation made it into the promised land. Consider those odds!

How many Christians do you know who do not regularly grumble and complain? Like the Israelites, we may have plenty of excuses, but God says no excuses are acceptable. He designed us for joy, and He sacrificed His Son to help us. Now it's up to us. If we prefer to disobey and live in unhappiness, the decision is ours; we will fail to experience the incredible joy that comes as we grow to trust God more and more. Hebrews 4:1 (TLB) tells us to tremble with fear because some of us may be on the verge of failing to enter His place of rest.

Reading this book could be your means of becoming the Caleb or Joshua who enters the promised land. If you have wasted precious energy thinking of your physical or emotional pains, try from this moment on to think new thoughts. You will be surprised and pleased to see how the Holy Spirit helps you have a new song in your heart.

The disciples practiced what they preached. Imprisoned, they sang at midnight. Then, great joy filled their thoughts and hearts. Like a fountain, it spilled over into the cold, dark cell. How did they do that? They did it through Christ.

God's Plans

God's goal is to prepare us to fellowship with Him for eternity. We must spend this life learning what we need to know. Otherwise we will not be equipped for our position and purpose in eternity. If I expend my energies praying for things I shouldn't have, God would defeat His own plans by honoring such prayers. Though our present bodies are frail, God decided that they perfectly suit His purpose. He takes our temporary bodies and uses them as places to work good in our eternal spirits.

I've learned that the most difficult task I must perform is to put God's plans first: "Seek first the kingdom of God" (Matt. 6:33). Our natural instinct is to take care of *our* families, *our* churches, *our* friends. Jesus' nature was to care for the people others shunned. At the end of this life, we will be judged according to the measure of our love for God and for people. It will profit us nothing to tell God about the sins we haven't committed or the miracles we have experienced. If we love ourselves too much, we will have little time and strength to love others.

Get It Done Yesterday

I'll share a truth with you that is worth one hundred times what you paid for this book.

Life often pressures us with the feeling that we must get things done immediately—if not sooner. Pressure can make us tense, irritable, resentful, confused. Sometimes we race as fast as we can go; other times we may give up and do nothing.

For many years I was accustomed to handling pressure in these ways until I heard a voice within: *Merlin, you have only one thing to do—please Me.* That was a revelation to my oft-troubled spirit. I had nothing else to do but please God. I remember and obey that message several times every day.

When I have a task to do that seems too time consuming, I remember that I have only one thing to do. When I feel pressured by some responsibility or some frustration, I'm able to rejoice when I remember that I can please God if I do my task with a joyful spirit.

Then I learned, now is the time I should please God. Not after a while. Not when I complete some task—*now*. When I center my attention on pleasing Him now, other responsibilities fade into the background. It is now that He wants me to be filled with peace.

One of the men on a cross beside Jesus could think only of his own physical condition. He had no interest in pleasing God now. So he challenged Jesus: "Get me off this cross!" The other man had a higher goal. His pain was just as great, but he asked Jesus to remember him when they entered the next world. His goal was right, and Jesus promised him he would attain it.

Remember these two men. The first asked for help to get off his cross, and he received nothing. The second asked to enter Christ's kingdom, and he received eternal life. Jesus didn't ask either of them to change his past, to do anything for Him, or to promise to do anything in the future. Both men needed help. Each had different priorities. One focused attention on his physical needs; the other sought the highest attainable goal—to be remembered in Jesus' kingdom.

You may find yourself as helpless as the thief on the cross. It may seem that you can do nothing to help yourself, which often results in fear.

Most men would like to be strong, but for some, building muscles is a top priority. Most women would like to be beautiful, but some make it their priority. If our priorities are out of balance, we are in spiritual jeopardy.

Putting the wrong things first is dangerous. God would like our physical bodies to be healed and all our problems solved. But He never puts our bodies first. No matter what we request, or what anyone tells us, our spiritual needs will always be most important to God.

God wants a bride for Christ that is without spot or wrinkle. A perfectly healthy body, unfortunately, might lead us in the opposite direction. When we think we have everything we need, we often have no great desire for God's help. That isn't God's fault or His choice; it is ours.

If a physician tells me I will die, the person I am at that moment determines how I will react. If death means I will lose everything that I have put first, I'm in bad shape. Serious illness is a master at creating fear. But it cannot defeat my faith in God if I have learned to put His will first. My body is not my first priority; therefore, it doesn't control me. Death becomes eternal joy and therefore works for my good. There is no way I can lose.

Jesus considered our priorities our most prized attributes. The rich young man who came to Him had a priority—money. Jesus told him to sell everything and give the money to poor people. That was too much for a man whose money had first place in his heart.

People who are blind often go through a time of intense discouragement. Healing could easily become their priority. I can understand that. But one man, Sydney Scroggle, achieved something that still stirs my enthusiasm. I copied one of his statements in my notebook, but I failed to list the title of his book or other important details about his life. I evidently believed and was blessed by what he wrote. I give you the quotation with the hope that it will encourage you in your efforts to have faith that God is working for good in your life. Scroggle wrote, "I came eventually to adopt an attitude towards blindness, resulting in freedom from all sense of restriction, feelings of self-pity, resentment, or embitterment. I cannot get anyone to believe me, but as others rejoice in their sight I rejoice in my blindness. It is purely and simply my own idea, that I would choose, had I a thousand alternatives." I am sure that Sydney struggled through and learned many things before he reached the freedom he described.

A Hospital in Vietnam

When I was a chaplain in Vietnam, wounded men were airlifted by helicopter to the evacuation hospital. It differed from hospitals you have visited. Buildings were of hastily erected corrugated metal, arranged in half-moon design, sitting on the ground or on cement slabs. Row after row of huts were full of wounded men. We received them within hours after they were injured.

War is a humbling experience, stripping most people of any smug pretense they may have. The awesome experience of war and ever-present death brought people face-to-face with themselves and their enemy, fear.

When I saw each casualty for the first time, I had no idea how serious the wounds might be. I might see only a small hole in the skin, made by a tiny fragment of steel. Appearances can be deceptive. The injury that didn't look like much could by the next morning be fatal.

As I stood by the bed of each newly arrived soldier, I realized that whatever I said might be the last words he would hear. I had no way of knowing what he needed most to hear or what his spiritual priorities had been. Many men were afraid; some were terrified. If a medical team was approaching, I knew it would be seconds before I had to leave.

Whatever I said needed to be in the right words. At times I sensed that my words expressed exactly what the particular soldier wanted to hear. As I went from bed to bed, I grasped each man's hand or touched some part of his body, and I said I was there to help. If he was strong enough, he would grip my hand. He might have never attended chapel, but he wanted to talk with someone who, to him, represented God. I was then able to tell him of times I, too, had been afraid and how I found peace through my faith in Jesus.

I spent most of my time at the EVAC hospital at the men's bedsides. Time after time I led men into personal relationships with Christ. The horror and stress of battle are long remembered, and I believe the survivors often recall how faith in God caused their fear to leave.

In those days I developed a passionate desire to help you be delivered from any stranglehold that fear may have on you Faith in God defeats, then destroys, all kinds of fear.

Now let us consider the different methods by which God urges us to believe Him.

CHAPTER 9

A Man of Great Faith

Jacob Van Gorder was born in New Jersey in 1761. In 1777, he was in the battle of the Tories and Native Americans against the settlers in Wyoming Valley, Pennsylvania. Native Americans captured him, but then a Native American woman adopted him as her son and saved his life.

After living with them for five years, he escaped while on a hunting party. Jacob is my ancestor; his genes are part of me.

My father, David, is still a part of my physical and spiritual makeup. He had never been confined to bed even one day until he died at age thirty-six. He had a beautiful wife and three healthy young sons. In his final year of laboring in the U.S. Steel Mill in Ellwood City, Pennsylvania, he was the highest paid hourly worker among thousands there.

Father's closest friend told me this unusual story: "The Sunday evening before your father died, he lingered at the church altar even after the lights were turned off. Finally only he and I were there. I said to him, 'Dave, do you have a problem?' He answered: 'I'm telling God that if necessary, I'm willing to die in order that my three sons might be saved.'"

In a few days my father died of pneumonia.

Those final days of his life profoundly influenced Mother. She knew that an angel had appeared to him just before he died, and that in some way his prayer for his three sons was important.

I was twelve years old when Mother came home from the hospital to tell us boys that he was dead. For the first time in my life I felt the kind of fear that can paralyze emotions. Even now I cannot describe how utterly alone I felt. I didn't cry or talk with anyone.

In our community the custom was to have the deceased at home in an open casket while for three days relatives and friends came to view the remains. Those days stand out in my mind as the worst of my life.

The open casket was in the living room that I had to pass through many times each day. Often no one was there but me and my lifeless father, and the sight of his corpse gave me nightmares for years to come. I don't recall seeing the flowers around the casket, but I do remember the smell of roses. To this day, when I smell roses, my mind flashes back to that scene so many years ago.

After the funeral, Mother said we couldn't pay the rent on our house and we would have to move.

Dad had an old car, but to me it was the most magnificent chariot on the road. He had let me sit in his lap to steer, and he promised a driver's license when I turned sixteen. When he worked on that old car, I always had my head in the way so I could see what he was doing. With his death, Mother had more bad news for us. The car had to go. She had no money for gasoline at twenty cents per gallon.

All those events were too severe for my young mind to accept. First Dad. Then the house. When we had to let the car go, I wondered what would be next. I soon found out. Mother said we must be very careful of the food we ate so we wouldn't run out.

I kept my eye on the kitchen and wondered if we would have something to eat for the next meal. Somehow we always managed to have cornmeal and beans, served with Mother's love, but to a son who was fearful and insecure.

I am sure that some of my readers have had more difficult times, but I share my experiences so you will know that I, too, know how it feels to be afraid. As you read this book, you may understand why you often felt fearful.

Golden Opportunities

At age fifteen, I found my world centered on playing football, baseball, and basketball, hunting, and a growing speculation about what girls were all about. At times I felt something within me urging me to seek God. I reacted as do many young people—I tried to keep Him from interfering with my life. To me, religion was for old people.

Yet, in one way or another God kept sending this word to me: *Merlin, you need to know Me.* One day I began to seek Him, and I soon wanted the whole world to know Him. He released in me an enthusiasm that overcame my inclination to be quiet and retiring.

If I attended church and the pastor said something that excited me, I would shout, "Praise the Lord!" unaware of what others around me were thinking. Later I learned of the disapproving comments some of the churchgoers made about my "vulgar display."

Fear of what people might say or think entered my heart. Then I learned the terrible secret: if I kept quiet, no one cared what I believed. The spiritual battle with fear had begun.

Eventually I stopped speaking to anyone about Jesus. Revelation 2:4 was written for me: "I have this against you, that you have left your first love." From age nineteen to age twenty-one I became a prodigal son and strayed far from God.

In my first book, *Prison to Praise,* I describe how God spoke to me when I was twenty-one. He said, *Tonight you must make a decision for Me. If you don't, it will be too late.* He was giving me my final opportunity to stay out of even more serious trouble than I had already experienced. I said yes, and He returned me to His service.

If you haven't been delivered from fearful thoughts, there's a very good chance that you, too, may be missing golden opportunities to influence others to accept Jesus as Savior. Your fear may be excused in dozens of ways:

- I don't know how.
- People would reject whatever I said.
- I'm naturally shy.
- I'm not trained.

I recall an incident that impressed itself forever on my mind. When I held the lowly rank of private in World War II, I was once in a formation with forty-eight men. We practiced the rifle manual of arms. Lieutenant Milam, a West Point graduate, shouted, "Right shoulder, arms; port arms; present arms." We were trained to fear all officers. One of them could say, "Sergeant, make that private work all weekend." Or worse, "That private disobeyed my direct order. Put him in the stockade."

Abruptly, Lieutenant Milam gave us "at ease." He was clearly upset by our performance. He said, "You men act as if you are too tired to move your eyeballs. What's wrong with you?

Put some life into what you're doing. Be proud you are paratroopers!"

Then: "There is only one of you who does this right. I'll bring him up here to show the rest of you lazy troopers the way it should be done."

Every man must have had the same thought: *Who is he talking about?*

"Private Carothers, come up here," he boomed in what I thought was an unnecessarily loud voice. I had to obey, but my feet didn't want to move. No sergeant, let alone an officer, had ever pointed me out as doing the manual of arms in an exemplary manner. Something terrible was about to happen.

With great trepidation I went up, expecting any minute to hear him laugh and say, "Carothers, you are a perfect example of the soldier who does this all wrong!"

However, he had me demonstrate all the elements of the drill, with flattering comments on my performance. I was in shock. It did not occur to me that I handled the rifle in a special way.

From then on, lieutenants were not to be feared. Rifle drills were fun. Everyone in the platoon watched to see how I did it, and the platoon sergeant looked on with obvious satisfaction. Lieutenant Milam was my hero, and I strove to please him.

That incident tells me that we are often needlessly afraid, and when fear enters the mind, it may take a dramatic experience to set us free of it. This has happened to me many times, as this book illustrates.

If someone had asked, "Carothers, do you care whether the officer in charge likes the way you do the manual of arms?" my answer would have been, "Do I care? Of course not." But I did care.

As you tell someone about eternal life, you want him or her

to react with pleasure and to show delight in listening to such a wonderful person as you. But you may also be afraid of how the person may react.

Matthew gave us an unusual report about a man who was not afraid: "When Jesus heard it, He marveled, and said to those who followed, 'Assuredly, I say to you, I have not found such great faith, not even in Israel!'" (Matt. 8:10).

Where did God's Son find the man of such great faith? His was not an occupation in which one would expect to find such faith. He was a soldier. Not Jewish, but Roman!

At age twelve, Jesus talked with the most religious people of His day. He later went to weddings, banquets, funerals, and talked with people wherever He went. But in all His lifetime He had not met one whose faith equaled that of the Roman soldier. What manner of man was he?

When Jesus located this soldier, He said, "I have not found such great faith," indicating that He had searched. To others, He said, "How is it that you have no faith?" (Mark 4:40); and "O you of little faith" (Matt. 6:30).

For many a day after that, the Roman officer surely was the subject of conversation among all those who followed Jesus. They must have asked, "Why is his faith so strong and ours so weak? How can we get more faith?"

I have heard many sermons about this Roman centurion. The emphasis is usually on his believing that Jesus did not need to go to his home in order to heal his servant. That was unusual faith, but there was a much stronger dimension of the soldier's faith. He called Jesus "Lord" (Greek, *kurios*). The primary use of this word in the New Testament is reliance upon Christ for salvation.

Roman law declared the emperor to be lord, and all persons were to have faith in him as lord. At the very least the officer subjected himself to loss of military rank. For what he had said, he could have been executed as a traitor.

A Roman soldier had every reason to deny Jesus as Lord. His position as a centurion meant wealth and power. If you have neither, you can hardly know how challenging it is for people to relinquish them. Power is usually difficult to attain, but even more difficult to abdicate. People often will sacrifice health, family, and integrity to gain and keep power.

The centurion probably spent years working to attain his status. Yet with a few words about Jesus, he laid himself open to lose everything, even his life. He risked everything, but for what? Not for personal gain. He didn't need healing for himself or his family; he didn't seek status. He wanted his servant to be healed.

In our culture that may not seem to be a big thing, but the servant of a Roman was as expendable as an animal would be. Both animals and servants had value, but they lived solely for their owner's convenience.

When you and I tell someone about our faith in Jesus, what do we jeopardize? Loss of earthly possessions? Or do we just risk being slightly embarrassed?

What caused the centurion to risk so much? Why was he unafraid when we are so often controlled by fear?

Jesus looked into the officer's heart, and He saw "great faith." We might miss the importance of what Jesus said if we do not understand the specific word chosen when He said "faith." What was the "great faith" that the officer had? The twelve disciples had already been out working miracles, yet not one of them was selected as having great faith. There is no indication in the account that the officer had done any work of faith. His faith was of a far superior variety. What was it?

Jesus said He had not found such great *pistis*. In Greek, it means "conviction of the truthfulness of God or a religious teacher." It is used here to mean believing on Christ for salvation. *Pistis* is used in this context throughout the New Testament.

Jesus said to the centurion, "As you have believed [*pisteuo*], so let it be done for you" (Matt. 8:13). The word means to have faith regarding a person, and by implication to entrust one's spiritual well-being to Christ.

Many people believed Jesus could work miracles, but He wasn't impressed by those who came seeking them. He was delighted with the centurion who was willing to risk his life by publicly announcing that he believed in Jesus as Lord.

There is more evidence that Jesus spoke about the centurion's faith in Him as Savior. In the next verse He said that "many will come from east and west, and sit down with Abraham, Isaac, and Jacob in the kingdom of heaven" (Matt. 8:11). Jesus would never have promised heaven to a man for simply believing that He could heal his servant. The eternal plan of salvation is based on one thing: faith in Jesus as Savior!

Not only did the Roman centurion believe in Jesus, but he was happy to witness to his faith. His confidence in Jesus, and his willingness to openly express his faith, marked him as one who believed more than any other man on earth! That touched Jesus so much that He marveled—considering it wonderful and astonishing.

Keeping Quiet

I have never told anyone that I was not a Christian. But because of fear, I often fail to express my faith. I find reasons strong enough to convince myself to keep quiet. Many times I would have acknowledged Jesus as Lord if my heart had not heard a whisper from the demon fear.

After Paul had been in prison for what some scholars believe to have been five years, he had good reason to hold his tongue. But he knew his mission and was prepared to die rather than be silent. They shackled him in prison for another five years. Ten years in a dungeon would dampen the enthusiasm of any man. Back on the streets, Paul still had but one message: *Jesus is our only hope of eternal life. He is alive! I saw Him with my own eyes. He is Lord.* They did not defeat him.

Back to prison he went for five more years. Fifteen or more years there did not change Paul's passion to tell the world about his Savior.

For nearly two thousand years people have searched for evidence that the New Testament record is not based on fact. Microscopic searches have been made through every scrap of evidence, with not one tiny flaw found. Not one! Unbelievers have ranted and raved, insisting, "He couldn't have risen from the dead." But He did! Jesus was the only One to conquer death.

In the forty days after His resurrection, many people saw Him. Those who proclaimed the holy event were beaten, tortured, stoned, fed to lions, or crucified, but they refused to recant. They were monumental proof that we serve a resurrected Jesus. Their sacrifice should inspire us to tell all people that He is alive.

In my lifetime, dozens of discoveries have verified the accuracy and reliability of the Bible. The media rarely report such revelations, but if one scrap of evidence were found to discredit Scripture, you can be sure that every branch of the news would feature it. If after two thousand years people found even one such fact, that would be news.

Unrelenting efforts are made to show Jesus as just another man. The apostles did not risk their lives preaching about just a good man. Jesus had the power to resurrect Himself from the dead, and they knew no ordinary man could do that.

Throughout history many men have promised to return from the dead, but not one has escaped the grave. Jesus was murdered, and just as He promised, He was raised from the dead. He appeared to hundreds of people, and as one astonished group watched, He ascended and disappeared into the sky.

He had said He would never leave them, but now He was gone. Those who had believed Him were in confusion. Some went back to their old jobs. Others met in small groups to await the possibility of further miraculous incidents. They did not know for certain what they waited for.

Something did happen! On the day of Pentecost, the church was born. Through the Holy Spirit, Jesus returned in a way that released the disciples from fear. Those believing in Him were charged with a new power and with a surge of passion to spread the joyful news. Those who had been afraid were no longer afraid. They rushed to tell the world, "He is alive! He is alive!"

Many believed them. Hundreds, then thousands of new believers rushed to tell others. Excited throngs poured out of Jerusalem, telling travelers, fishermen, soldiers—everyone who would listen—that Jesus was alive.

Roman authorities saw things were getting out of hand because Caesar was considered a god. No man was to be worshiped other than the emperor. Commands went out. Anyone who claimed that Jesus Christ was alive would be fed to the lions. Many believers were murdered, but a strange thing happened. When two believers were slain, four would take their place. Nothing seemed to stop them.

But something did! Eventually new believers became afraid

to tell anyone. Persecution decreased. Believers relaxed. No need to stir up trouble.

But the good news survived. Stronger and bolder Christians kept passing along the secret. One day you and I heard it. When we did, God sowed a seed in our hearts that helps us to be a part of His miracle. Working with Him we accomplish the impossible!

Hudson Taylor, one of the greatest missionaries of all time, said, "There are three stages in every great work of God. First, it is impossible, then it is difficult, then it is done."

Multitudes of Christians become tongue-tied when they have an opportunity to share Christ with unbelievers. The desire to avoid problems that come to them as a result of speaking up about Christ is stronger than the desire to communicate.

Christians often berate themselves unmercifully for failing to obey Christ. They feel defeated, discouraged, and wonder why they are such miserable examples of true discipleship. They read books about witnessing, attend classes, and listen to sermons, but the problem remains unresolved.

What is wrong? The basic cause is not being considered—only the symptoms.

We can pray 10 times a day, 3,650 times a year for 50 years, for the strength to be a faithful witness and still fail. Why? Because we allow ourselves to be divided. Jesus said, "[A] house divided against itself will not stand" (Matt. 12:25).

God has given each of us the power to cast out the fear of being a witness. We may need to do this over and over until we grasp the meaning of these verses: "If the Son makes you free, you shall be free indeed" (John 8:36); and "Where the Spirit of the Lord is, there is liberty" (2 Cor. 3:17).

It doesn't take too much persuasion for most of us to muster up a good strong desire for an ice-cream sundae. By applying God's Word we can learn to desire to tell others about our Savior. The desire to build God's kingdom and the desire to stand back and escape responsibility are mutually exclusive. Waiting for someone else to initiate action usually indicates a lack of confidence in ourselves and in God. We can pray every day for confidence and never feel it. Self-confidence is often unable to overcome fear, but unfailing confidence comes as we learn to cast fear from our hearts and minds.

Obedience

Many Christians lose spiritual battles because they let a spirit of defeat control their actions rather than stand on God's promises. Many Christians repeat, "I can do all things," over and over. They sing it, pray it, even try to do it, but they fail if they live in a "house divided against itself." Faith lives in one room, but fear controls the rest of the house.

The power of Christ's life rested in His decision to follow God's will. His miracles would never have redeemed you and me. His obedience to God provided our salvation. Our obedience makes us workers with Him.

When people first began to report Jesus as alive, they gave their testimonies so fearlessly that all unbelievers knew that if they became believers, they, too, would go about telling others of the power of Jesus to save. That's all too often not true today. Many Christians have been infected by the timorous behavior of other Christians. Thus, they often think it proper to be secret believers. The results are tragic. Many converts never know the joy of telling others the good news, and their gladness of heart quickly dissipates.

Place a drop of blue ink in a glass of water, and the entire contents will turn blue. Just one drop. Let one drop of fear be in your heart, and it will permeate everything in you. Therefore, you must find ways to eliminate those drops of fear. I dedicate this book to help you achieve that goal.

CHAPTER 10

Don't Be Manipulated

When people don't believe that God is actively involved in their lives, they find endless reasons to be afraid. If faith in God declines, they then dwell on fears.

Some may wonder if Christians are being gullible by putting their confidence and trust in a God they can't see. So let's think about what we can see.

Picture the sky divided into thousands of windows the size of the moon as we see it. With a giant telescope, let's zoom in and examine one of these windows. If our telescope is powerful enough, we will see not only individual stars but also galaxies.

How many stars are in each galaxy? Astronomers say there are two hundred billion to five hundred billion, each at least a million times larger than the earth.

The reality of it staggers the mind. The space between stars is even more mind-boggling.

Consider a short trip from the earth to the nearest star, excluding the sun. If we could travel there by car on a smooth highway and we averaged one thousand miles a day, it would take three million years to get there.

Other stars are 20 billion light-years away, each distance equal to 186,000 miles per second, times 60 seconds per minute, times 60 minutes per hour, times 24 hours per day, times 365 days, times 20 billion years. Think of all that empty space out there!

Galaxies whirl through space at tens of thousands of miles per hour to cross the universe in magnificent order. Billions upon billions of stars sweep through the universe, seemingly in perfect harmony.

How many galaxies are there? In 1996 the Hubble Space Telescope increased the estimated number to *fifty billion*. That is five times as many as previously estimated!

Our own Milky Way, considered to be an ordinary galaxy, has an estimated fifty to one hundred billion stars. Multiply fifty billion galaxies by one hundred billion per galaxy to get the possible number of stars!

An atom is a "universe" equal in complexity to the entire universe. The human mind is incredible. Yet in all of history we have never once created anything. All we do is rearrange the atoms we have.

Ask an atheist to explain the origin of our vast universe. Of all the learned people who have lived, not one has a vague idea of how matter and energy were created to compose those billions of stars.

Proponents of evolution say everything evolved. To believe that the universe gradually appeared out of nothing seems to require a kind of madness that is beyond comprehension—unless there was a Creator.

Even after I was a Christian I spent years pleading with the Creator to show Himself: "God, why don't You reveal Yourself? Don't You want us to trust You? Why do You keep us in the dark?" The more doubt I expressed, the stronger it became. Doubt begets more doubt.

Then God ignited a spark of faith in me and challenged me to do something with that spark. I could let it go out, or I could fan it into a flame that could release more faith. Now, I know it is illogical to doubt God's existence. To believe that He created all things is the only rational conclusion that any thoughtful person has ever reached. It's no wonder that we want to shout to the world, "God is for real!"

Paul's faith in God was so strong that he continued preaching even when he knew his message would cause him to be put into prison or even be executed. His faith gave him the power to write chapters in a book that was to be published by God. Noted scholar H. L. Hastings wrote,

> Infidels for 1,800 years have refuted and overthrown this book, and yet it stands today as solid as a rock. Its circulation increases, and it is more loved, cherished, and read today than ever before. Infidels, with all their assaults on this book, make about as much impression on it as a man with a tack hammer would on the pyramids of Egypt. When the French monarch proposed the persecution of Christians in his dominion, an old statesman and warrior said to him, "Sire, the Church of God is an anvil that has worn out many hammers." So, for ages the hammers of infidels have been pecking away at this book, but are now worn out and the anvil still endures. If it had not been the book of God, men would have destroyed it long ago. Emperors and popes, kings and priests, princes and rulers have all tried their hands at it; they die and the book still lives.

For many years, so-called higher critics assured student pastors in liberal seminaries that Moses could not possibly have written the first five books of the Bible. Why? They said there was no such thing as the writing of *anything* when Moses lived. End of discussion.

Then the written laws of Hammurabi were discovered. To the consternation of the higher critics, those detailed laws proved to have been written three hundred years before Moses lived.

Critics have sniped at any and every tiny detail in the Bible to try to prove it unreliable. In *Archaeology of Palestine,* William F. Albright, long recognized as a great archaeologist, writes of it: "Discovery after discovery has established the accuracy of innumerable details, and has brought increased recognition of the value of the Bible as a source of history."

A few historians have dismissed Jesus as a historical figure. They say, "We cannot accept the Bible's word that Jesus lived." If you should encounter an unbeliever who asks you, "How can you be sure that Jesus ever lived?" you can assure the person that no qualified historian would consider Jesus a myth. Not even considering the Bible, there is far more evidence that Jesus lived than there is for the existence of Shakespeare.

Many who need help, but do not know who Jesus is, see no verification that God has ever done anything to help them. They do not see evidence that anyone in the world can help them or that anyone even cares. Such an outlook becomes fertile ground for fear.

Your fear may be different. You may nourish a hope that God has been with you, yet remember times when He didn't answer your prayers. You feel as though you have been knocked about by life. If something bad could happen, it did. (That's Murphy's Law in full force!)

You doubt that you have been good enough for God to intervene in your life or that you ever will be good enough. That leaves ample reason to face the future with fear.

Why Doesn't God Help Me?

Why doesn't God solve our problems right away when we sincerely seek His help? I had a vision that helped me to better understand.

I saw a pool table with multicolored balls scattered about. However, one was different. It had the letter M printed all over it. The ball had to get to a white spot on the table for the game to end.

The cue stick hit the M ball and sent it crashing into the colored balls, which then careened back and forth across the table. The M ball was bounced back and forth by the movement of all the others. It would stop close to the white spot but never on it. Close was not good enough, and the game seemed endless. I thought, *Why does this game go on and on? The M ball will never stop exactly on the tiny white spot. What can be the purpose of this?*

None of it made sense. I wanted to pick up the ball and place it on the white spot. As my hand moved to do so, the entire scene disappeared.

As I thought about what I had seen, I began to understand. The M ball was for Merlin. As in the game, God has an exact spot at which He wants Merlin to be. He has used many forces to influence my life. Although I didn't see His hand, He caused or permitted experiences to move me from one situation to another. He touched the life of one person, who in turn touched someone else, who in turn would touch my life. Now I'm sure that He has always been involved.

Sometimes I've felt like shouting, "What's the point of my being knocked back and forth all over the place when You could easily put me exactly where You want me to be?"

Some experiences have been delightful, some miserable. But every one of them had the same purpose: to get me where I needed to be. With this perspective, the misfortunes in my past are no longer painful memories.

When you feel manipulated by experiences that make no sense to you, picture the pool table I mentioned, and see your name on one of the balls. Don't be dismayed by the things that people do or don't do to you. People and circumstances may be able to move you from one place to another. But people cannot control your reactions. Only you can do that. If you decide to be angry, resentful, or bitter, it may take a long time to get you moved to the place you need to be.

Whatever people do for us—or against us—will be used by God to move us to His chosen place, once we learn to trust Him. If we need to be embarrassed, someone will come along to take care of our need. Remember the verse: "God shall supply all your need according to His riches in glory by Christ Jesus" (Phil. 4:19). He always causes things to happen to meet our needs. He holds the cue stick.

He sees the sparrow that falls. He knows how many hairs are on our heads. Nothing—absolutely nothing—can happen without His knowledge. Our faith in His control defeats all kinds of fear.

Steve Largent, a professional football player with the Seattle Seahawks, put it this way: "I thank God I never had it easy. He's the One who built that obstacle course, who set up the hurdles, in order for me to grow."

Steve faced many obstacles, yet continued to do his best. In high school the coach told Steve he was too small and too slow to be good at football. But he loved football, so he kept working, kept improving his skills.

When he sought college scholarships, time after time Steve was told the same thing; he was too small and too slow. Steve kept working and believing that God would help him over the seemingly insurmountable obstacles. Finally, Tulsa University awarded him a scholarship. In his junior and senior years he led the nation in touchdown catches.

Are you backed into a corner with some problem? Do you feel alone and helpless? Jesus promised, "Lo, I am with you always, even to the end of the age" (Matt. 28:20).

Fear tries to say, "You are alone and helpless." But faith says, "God is with me!"

CHAPTER 11

Unfair Predicaments

It came as a wonderful relief when I first accepted the fact that I would never be perfect.

When people find fault with us, they can easily irritate us. Most of us have a craving to be perfect and to have everyone realize our perfection. But we are not, and we never will be.

When people point out our imperfections, we do not need to be hurt. Instead, we can find ways to make their opinions work something good in us. That way, whatever people say about us, we are bound to profit.

Understanding my imperfections made it much easier for me to accept the things people said about me. A big burden rolled off my shoulders. I came to see why Paul wrote so freely about his imperfections. He said, "Christ Jesus came into the world to save sinners, of whom I am chief" (1 Tim. 1:15).

We are distracted from what God thinks of us if other people's opinions upset us. It is pleasing to God if we can hear a derogatory opinion sent our way, and we react with this confidence: "God, I know You will work this for my good." Of course, we can often profit from constructive criticism, but we need to put God's opinion at the very center of our concerns.

We often respond to criticism in such a negative way that we cannot profit from it. But if we value God's opinion so highly that we turn criticism over to Him, He will then help us to profit from all the good or bad things that people say about us. Taking that approach will make life so much easier to live.

During my lifetime, I seemed to be backed into many corners with no way out, no relief in sight, no one to help. I felt utterly helpless, yet help came. As I look back on those experiences, one factor stands out: each time I learned something new. In some way I became stronger, growing in the realization that Someone was on my side, watching for the right moment to come to my aid.

A Serious Illness

During some of my most difficult experiences, it seemed that God allowed me to be pushed into unfair predicaments.

Once my wife, Mary, was seriously ill, in horrendous pain. We cried out to God for a healing miracle. He had healed us of other infirmities, but that time our prayers and those of hundreds of other loving people produced nothing—or so we thought. Mary's condition worsened. She became so ill that she couldn't dress or wash herself, sit, stand up, or even lie in bed without severe pain. My fears escalated.

The Lord asked me a question that posed an agonizing dilemma: If I had only one prayer to be answered, would I ask Him to heal Mary, or would I ask Him to help us get permission to distribute 250,000 copies of a condensed version of *Prison to Praise*? What a question! For months we had pleaded with the publisher to give us permission to do the printing. I knew that such a massive distribution could lead many people to eternal life. But more than anything I could ask for myself, I desperately wanted Mary to be healed. Her suffering tortured me.

In my agony I had to tell God I wanted Him to help us get permission to print the 250,000 condensed copies of *Prison to Praise*. We got permission, printed them, and sent copies to the darkest corners of the world. That was fourteen years ago, and we are still receiving word about people accepting Jesus as they read it.

Mary was still hurting, and I died inside as I watched her suffer. Her pain spread to nearly every movable joint. The specialist shook his head and predicted a lifetime using a wheelchair, receiving medications that would give only partial relief. How Satan must have smiled!

A few persons hinted that Mary must have some hidden sin in her life. God must have been grieved; I surely was.

We traveled to Mexico seeking help, read dozens of books, tried many things. Our confidence in God was pushed to the limit. At times my trust alternated between faith and fear, but we held fast: "God, You will help us. You will! We praise You through our tears. You *are* working this for good."

He answered! Not with a miracle healing, but with a natural remedy that eventually removed 95 percent of Mary's pain. The remedy to which He led us is not for everyone. It probably would be ineffective for many people with the same problem. What is important is that God led us to the solution. All of us have vital lessons we must learn along our way. The journey may be even more important than reaching the destination.

Not only did we print all those copies of the special edition of *Prison to Praise*, but something else that was beyond our expectations happened—something we hadn't dreamed of asking God to do.

California Bound

On our cross-country trek to California in 1972, Mary and I had the wonderful opportunity to spend several days with friends in Moran, Wyoming. There we met Pete and Gretchen Finch. Gretchen arranged a praise meeting to be held in their home. Pete told me later that he had not been happy about having a preacher in his home.

The meeting was one of those extra-special times. As a result, Pete received Jesus as his Savior, became an enthusiastic student of the Bible, and later pastored a church.

Years later I conducted meetings in that area and again stayed with the Finches. Pete took me on a horseback ride into the magnificent Grand Tetons around Moran and Jackson Hole. That part of God's world must please Him very much. The mountains reach high into the sky, and the valleys are treasure lands of pure beauty. God's wondrous creation seemed to create a deep feeling of peace in my heart.

While enjoying our friends' hospitality, I became acquainted with an attorney who also was a guest. As I reluctantly prepared to leave for home, he said, "Merlin, my office is in New Jersey. If you ever need legal help in that part of the country, please call me." Legal help in New Jersey? Why would I ever need that? Yet I would learn that God often brings into our lives people and events that at the time seem of little significance.

Sometime after we printed the special edition of *Prison to Praise,* I received some bad news. The publisher of my books had declared bankruptcy. The printing of our books would stop, with legal proceedings that could go on for months or years. Would the message of praise to God be put on hold for months? How could that possibly be a part of His plan?

One day as I worked at thanking the Lord for the new

problem, the remark of the New Jersey attorney flashed into my mind. The publishing firm was in New Jersey. Looking through my notes for his number, I wondered if he was still there. He was. He said he would look into the matter, and he soon called back.

"Merlin, I have good news. We can do better than getting permission for you to print your books. I believe we can get the publishing rights back in your name." Back in my name? I had no idea such a thing could be done. In a few days the attorney called to ask if I could come to New Jersey to the courthouse to meet with the attorney named by the court as trustee. We could talk during the bankruptcy hearings. You can imagine how quickly I said yes.

At the courthouse we met during a recess with the trustee. In a few minutes he was back in court and addressed the judge: "Your honor, I recommend that the publishing rights for the books by Merlin R. Carothers be given to him."

"So ordered."

"What do we do next?" I asked the trustee.

"Nothing. It's all done. The books are yours. You can do whatever you want with them."

My vision had been only big enough to ask God to help us get permission to print a special edition of one book. But He made it possible to continue printing all of the praise books.

Our entire ministry was revolutionized. Previously we had paid the publisher twice the printing cost for the books we donated to people in the service, hospital patients, and prisoners. Now we could print hundreds of thousands of copies at the lowest rates available. My faith took a giant leap forward. Millions of people could be reached! My lifelong vision of evangelizing the world, one at a time or by the millions, was a step closer. And I was one step closer to understanding why God wants us to be delivered from fear.

Reaching the World

What prevents millions of people from becoming Christians today? Is it greed, lust, pleasure, indifference, or what? What would cause millions of men and women to make personal decisions to forsake all and follow Christ this year? More churches, more Bibles? More Christian television, books, dedicated pastors, even great catastrophes? Or would it require multiple, clearly irrefutable miracles?

The answer is simple. None of the above!

God sent His Son to the earth with His plan. Jesus gave us the formula, but something has gone amiss. Fear prevents the good news of salvation by faith in Jesus from being shared with every person in our nation and the world. Let me emphasize the word *fear*.

Our greatest need is not for more finances, expensive tools, or more classes on how to evangelize. I had courses in college and seminary on all the techniques, and I have read many well-written books on the subject. I've conducted many classes and inspired thousands of Christians to go out into the community with the message that had brought eternal life to each of them. These things are useful, but knowing what to say or how to say it will never cause any of us to overcome our fears.

Fear can bind us as powerfully as do prison isolation cells. It can destroy communication as effectively as cutting out the tongue. Fear paralyzes the following:

- Good intentions
- Enthusiasm

- Determination
- Zeal and passion to tell others about our Savior

Shakespeare wrote, "Our fears do make us traitors."

After Jesus was arrested, Peter had a prime opportunity to tell others about Him. But he was so intimidated that he cursed, and he swore he didn't know Him.

I'm thankful that Peter failed so miserably. He gives us a clear picture of what we all will do if we allow fear to control us. Perhaps we won't curse and swear that we don't know Him, but we may act as if we don't.

Please remember this: Jesus is as alive today as He was when Peter denied knowing Him. He sees what we do when we have opportunities to tell others that He is our friend.

Wherever we go, we leave a part of ourselves, and God gives us the incredible ability to influence the eternal destinies of our fellow human beings.

Take a walk down a street, across a road, and into a forest where you follow no pathway. Walk for five, ten, or twenty miles, being careful to leave no trail. Leave no evidence that you have passed that way.

Twenty-four hours later a well-trained dog can follow your trail. How? Not by sight, for you left no visible trail. He puts his nose to the ground and sniffs the scent you left there and in the air. He smells not only your shoes, but your distinctive scent that went through them to the ground. You weren't aware of leaving anything behind, but you did.

Lukewarm believers are fearful and silent, but we are told to be bold in spirit. We are to speak up, to witness, to leave our mark.

In Jesus' parable of the talents (Matt. 25 TLB), one servant was given $5,000, another $2,000, the third $1,000. The man who received $1,000 hid it in the ground; he was afraid to use it.

If you think of yourself as untalented, and you justify hiding your talents, Jesus says to you, "The man who uses well what he is given shall be given more, and he shall have abundance. But from the man who is unfaithful, even what little responsibility he has shall be taken from him" (Matt. 25:29 TLB).

I've encouraged many people to use the simple talent of being able to speak into a telephone. Help organize a survey through your church. Then call people listed in your local telephone book. Introduce yourself in whatever way seems comfortable to you. You might say, "I'm a member of the XYZ church, and I'm making a survey. I'm not asking you to attend our church. I just want your opinion. What do you think a person needs to do in order to go to heaven?"

Once you discover that people do not understand the good news of the gospel, you may be able to share the good news with them. Some folks are using this method so successfully that they are leading someone to Christ on an average of one *every day*!

Now let's consider what makes a church.

CHAPTER 12

What Makes a Church?

Fear should never cause us to allow people with many or great talents to do all the work of sharing the good news. Here is a sequence that is too often repeated:

Two bold, courageous, unafraid Christians meet and discuss their mutual desire to bring men and women to Christ. They bring two others to Him.

Now, four unafraid, zealous Christians go out and win four others. Soon they are eight, sixteen, thirty-two, and sixty-four in number.

One man becomes the pastor. A beautiful church building is erected and dedicated to bringing men and women to Christ. The pastor is declared responsible for keeping the church organized. During the week, he meets with many leaders from within its fold.

The choir director stresses the need for new choir members and urges the pastor to mention this "next Sunday." The Sunday school superintendent urges the pastor to plead for teachers "next Sunday." The youth director pleads for him to urge members to help with the youth activities "next Sunday."

The most emotional plea of all comes from the treasurer. He tells the pastor that unless he inspires people to give more, the budget in every department in the church must be cut. This is not good news. Everyone is afraid that something must be done.

When the pastor steps to the pulpit Sunday morning, his mind is crammed with all the programs he must push. He thinks, *What if I fail?* Everything must be squeezed into the one hour allotted to him by his sheep. He can't cut any of the sacred moments given to the choir or music director. He can't shortchange any special projects. If the people don't give their tithes, the entire church will collapse.

So, he urges the congregation to contribute to all these good and important things. The church supports itself. There is some mention of the need to reach the unsaved, but that isn't the heart and soul of the church. The pastor, his assistants, the elders, and the heads of each department have as their first priority its preservation.

The church may temporarily increase in attendance. Its people will doubtless appreciate its youth programs, nursery, well-organized Sunday school, choir, and inspiring sermons. But the people have stopped witnessing for Christ and soon become afraid to do so.

If this scenario were typical of only one church in a community, the results would not be fatal. But when many churches become centered only on supporting themselves, the spirit of evangelism gradually dies. They become places to meet and eat, mere social clubs. Winning people to Christ and taking care of them are inseparable, but each must be kept in balance if the church is to reach its divine objective.

My own denomination, Methodism, was once a flaming fire of evangelism. Converts were trained to go out and win others.

People who had a passion for reaching the lost were placed in charge of people who wanted to reach others. Anyone who was afraid of being beaten, stoned, or put into prison was never appointed as a teacher or preacher. Their enthusiasm and refusal to be afraid caused Methodists to reach across England, Colonial America, and ultimately the world. The ardent evangelists met in fields, forests, and brush arbors. They were exhorted to share the good news of the gospel with everyone in the world.

Their leader, John Wesley, did not want to start a denomination; his burning passion was to win more souls to Christ. John frequently walked straight toward mobs screaming that he should be killed. The 110-pound giant was often characterized as the man who knew no fear.

John's fearless stance caused him to become my hero. When I've faced situations that could have made me fearful, I've remembered John.

When I was assigned as pastor of a Methodist circuit in 1948, one of the churches looked terrible. It hadn't been painted for so long that the paint was barely visible. When I asked why it hadn't been painted, I was told, "There are two factions in the church. They can never agree on how the necessary money is to be raised, and so nothing is ever done."

On one side was a man who was known as the financial pillar of the church. Many people looked to him to take care of most of the church's financial needs. The people were always afraid of his being offended. A smaller group resented the man's control over everything in the church, so they refused to cooperate with anything that he wanted.

I went to visit the financial pillar. When I arrived at his farm, he was in the barn shoveling manure with a pitchfork. During our conversation, he told me what should be done to raise the money to paint the church. I said, "No, that's not what I am going to do." That was not what he expected to hear from a new, young preacher. He stopped his work, held his pitchfork in front of him, and walked straight at me.

He said, "Yes, you will, or you're finished." I stood my ground and focused on his eyes. He was furious. Fire and brimstone stoked his rage. I had heard that he was used to ministers doing whatever he said. If they didn't, he would take whatever actions he considered appropriate.

Of course, I had reason to be afraid. The man was obviously unpredictable, and I was barely beginning in my long journey of going from fear to faith. As I stood my ground, I remembered John Wesley. His courage inspired me. I moved toward the seething church pillar. But I couldn't go far because the prongs of the pitchfork came right to my throat. The next few minutes seemed to last forever, but he saw that I wasn't going to back down. You may be sure that I was relieved when he lowered the pitchfork, told me to leave, turned his back, and went back to work.

The next Sunday I told the congregation the decision I had made regarding the painting of the church: "Raising funds will not be necessary. I'll be here ready to work next Saturday morning at 6:00 A.M. with a bucket of paint. Anyone who wants to help, please bring your paintbrush."

One man spoke up, "But what about the steeple? You can't paint it. It's too high. We need professionals for that." And it was high.

"I'll paint it," this bold young man said, although I had never before painted a building, let alone a church steeple. All that week I was tempted to worry about the steeple that had obviously been built to reach into the heavens.

Saturday morning, to my immense delight, twelve men

showed up to help the preacher. But before they began, they wanted to see how I intended to paint the steeple that was too high for any ladder to reach.

"Lord, what do I do now?" Then I saw a picture in my mind of being trained how to blow up bridges. *That's it, I* thought. *God arranged for me to be in Demolitions School so I would know how to paint a church steeple!* Isn't God clever? I rigged ropes over the steeple so I could hang from the top and paint.

From then on I was a hero to nearly every man in the church. They started bringing new men "to see the new preacher." Money poured in to pay for everything we needed, and even more than we needed. Attendance increased and was soon doubled. Nearly every week someone came forward to receive Jesus as Savior.

The church lost the financial pillar, but members didn't seem to mind. Fear takes a backseat when faith controls our actions.

Evangelical Fervor

Fear caused the original evangelical fervor of Christians in our country to be replaced by a survival mentality. This attitude causes us to lose sight of our primary mission. When church members do not birth Christians, stagnation and decay set in.

Have you ever seen a woman's eyes light up when she sees someone else's baby? She wants to hold and gaze at it in rapt attention. Often her first thought is, *I want a baby!* The sight of mother and child causes her to want to bear her own child.

The enthusiasm of new converts inspires other Christians. They want to go out and birth converts on their own. Victories beget new victories.

I am increasingly enthusiastic as I realize what can happen if we regain our potential to influence the people of the world. You may be a young person with no experience or training or a mature adult with many talents. You may be an older citizen on a fixed income or a successful executive. You may have nearly perfect health or use a wheelchair. Whatever your status or condition in life, you have unlimited potential to persuade others to receive Jesus as their Lord and Savior. You and I have the exalted opportunity to allow God to speak through us. We have only one problem. If we are afraid, God will find someone else to do His work.

To His followers, Jesus said, "Tell the good news to every nation and to every person." If everyone in the world who believes in Jesus as Savior would lead one person to Christ each year (not one per day or one per month, just one per year), how long do you think it would take to win the world to Him? Not many years.

The *World Christian Encyclopedia* indicates that there are now more than 1.5 billion Christians in the world today. What if just 3 percent of them could be delivered from the terrible shackles of fear, able to spend a few minutes a day telling other people the good news? That would amount to 50 million working, active Christians. If each birthed one active Christian, next year there would be 100 million. Results would continue in this way:

2d year—200 million
3d year—400 million
4th year—800 million
5th year—1 billion, 600 million
6th year—3 billion, 200 million
7th year—6 billion, 400 million

Satan is well aware of this potential. He heard Jesus say, "Preach the gospel to every creature," and he knows that he must silence the mouths of believers.

Jesus spent His final moments here on earth urging us to go and tell all people the good news. When everything is ready, He will return. What is the exact date of His return? I'm about to tell you exactly when.

What is His plan? Romans 11:25 supplies the clearest answer that I see in the entire Bible: "Blindness in part has happened to Israel until the fullness of the Gentiles has come in."

What a challenge! What a reason to build God's kingdom with every ounce of our strength! When the full number of Gentiles is complete, Jesus will descend from heaven with a shout! To me, that means He waits for us to complete *our* assignment. When we complete that task, He will claim His throne here on earth. He wants to end wars, suffering, and pain, but He will wait for us to complete our assignment.

On Trial

The court is in session and the trial in progress. Everyone focuses attention on the witness. The judge, jury, prosecuting and defense attorneys, bailiff, and court and news reporters wait expectantly. Everyone wants to know, "What will the witness say? Will he verify the prosecuting attorney's claims or those of the defendant?"

For now, the witness is the center of attention. The outcome of the trial depends on what he says.

He is silent. Everyone leans forward in anticipation of what he may say. He remains silent.

The judge is impatient. "Answer the question, please."

Still the witness says nothing. Reporters poise their pencils.

The jury stirs impatiently, wondering why the witness hasn't spoken.

Finally the judge says, "Sir, either you must answer the question, or I must hold you in contempt."

That's it! A witness who is too afraid to speak can be held in contempt. God asks us, "And how can they hear about him unless someone tells them?" (Rom. 10:14 TLB). If 10 percent of readers of this book were inspired to cast off the shackles of fear, we could unite to bring hundreds of millions of people to Christ.

Fewer than 10 percent of the people of Russia brought that vast country under communism. The 10 percent brought billions of other people under the ruthless control of atheism. In our own United States, 10 percent of the membership of political parties controls them. Ten percent of all Christians could bring a spiritual awakening to the world!

You may be tempted to think, *I'm just one person. There is little I can do to change the world.* Most of us don't have an opportunity to speak to millions of people, but when we tell anyone about our faith in God, we have His power behind us. Our mouths can speak His words and carry the strength of His power.

Here is a bold, brash estimate: 95 percent of unbelievers in the United States have never heard the good news that we receive the free gift of eternal life simply by inviting Jesus to be our Lord and Savior. Why? The good news is preached in churches, where few unbelievers attend, on Christian television programs that unbelievers seldom watch, and in books that unbelievers can ignore if they choose. Unbelievers have little cause to be concerned with the good news we are reporting. They never hear it.

Jesus defeated Satan's master plan to hold the entire human

race in slavery. Then He placed the completion of His plan in our hands. What a magnificent calling we have!

Olympic Contenders

Fear, even in the most minute proportion, can defeat the loftiest ambitions. After the Olympics I listened to interviews with gold medalists. Contestants were asked if they expected to win. Winners always answered yes. They always expect to win. The contenders said their attitudes had to be perfect as they stepped up to the starting line. One negative feeling could destroy a lifetime of preparation for the Olympics. They could think no negative thoughts. None!

You may think, *How could it be possible to not think a thought if that thought came into your mind?* Olympic contenders must learn to control what comes to their minds, or they don't win.

Paul stated that we are in a race. We are to run it as if we expect to win. If fear enters our minds, we will fail. Other people may have to pay the price for our failures. They miss the gift of eternal life. And we forfeit the reward of our Father's saying, "Well done, good and faithful servant" (Matt. 25:21).

The church is the army of the Lord. Armies often are destroyed because the soldiers are afraid. The annals of warfare are filled with accounts of entire armies put to flight not by the enemy, but by fear. If one man in the front ranks turns and flees toward the rear, he can cause an undisciplined horde to panic with him.

From the first day a man enters military service, the main order of business is to teach him to be disciplined. Every drill and marching order is designed to instill rigid conformity. Each soldier must put his left foot forward in exact unison with ninety-nine comrades. Each must start, turn, reverse directions, run, or stop, all in harmony with the rest. Every minute of the day he is trained to respond only to orders. After many months of severe discipline, he begins to respond to every command as though it was his own idea. Stubborn vestiges of fear may lurk within him, but rigorous discipline, consistently imposed, increases the likelihood that he will respond in a disciplined manner.

God calls us to a disciplined life: "[We are to bring] every thought into captivity to the obedience of Christ" (2 Cor. 10:5); and "Those who are Christ's have crucified the flesh with its passions and desires. If we live in the Spirit, let us also walk in the Spirit" (Gal. 5:24–25).

CHAPTER 13

A Nugget of Pure Gold

For more than forty-nine years I have written and talked about faith. Now, at age seventy-two, I have a clearer understanding of how faith should work in everyday life. If I can help you to understand, I will rejoice.

I wasn't thinking about Abraham, but the thought came to me: *Abraham believed God, and it was accounted to him for righteousness* (Rom. 4:3).

A question formed in my mind: *What did Abraham do that caused God to credit him with righteousness?* My answer was, *He believed God.*

Then came the question, *How long did Abraham believe God?* And the answer: *For many years.*

Keep thinking about that.

As I meditated, a light suddenly turned on in my mind. Something important, *really* important, had been revealed to me.

God told Abraham to travel into a strange country, without knowing where he was going or why. He was told to leave his old associations and to go into new territory. Abraham was seventy-five when the Lord told him to leave Haran. He headed south toward the land of the Canaanites, on to Egypt, then back up to the land of Canaan. The long walk extended to more than one thousand miles. It was indeed a faith tour.

Travel, Abraham style, involved walking with his wife and all his goats, sheep, and donkeys. Animals move slowly and want to eat something nearly every step of the way.

Abraham and his family carried their tents and set up camp whenever they paused. Imagine yourself going to bed in a strange desert. When you wake up the next morning, you try to plan your day, but there is only one thing to do. Keep walking toward an unknown destination, over land you have never seen, until God gives you some signal that it is time to stop. Will there be food and water? What enemies lie out there waiting to attack? For how many days could you trudge onward without knowing where you are or where you are going? Abraham refused to turn back. Each day, and perhaps every hour, he had to renew his decision to walk by faith.

When Abraham was one hundred and Sarah ninety, God rewarded their walk of faith. Up to that time they had no children, although He had promised them that their descendants would be as numerous as the stars.

Some years after Isaac was born, a greater test of faith came to Abraham. God told him to kill his beloved son. Not giving Abraham more children as He had promised, He was taking his only son. And Abraham continued to believe that God would keep His promise.

As I meditated on Abraham's faith, the Holy Spirit opened my understanding. Before this experience, I had always believed there was something wrong with my faith if I prayed and nothing happened. Have you done the same? I felt that God must be displeased with me, though I didn't know why.

When a Scripture verse, a sermon, or someone's testimony stimulated my faith, I would try again to believe that God had answered my prayer. If nothing worthwhile happened, I would again become discouraged. Does this sound familiar?

When I prayed for physical healing, I was susceptible to giving up. In desperation I would pray, fast, and study Bible verses on faith. Then I would try to stretch my faith as far as I could. If nothing happened, I would slip back into a feeling of defeat.

Abraham didn't pray and believe that way. He kept on believing. As the years passed, he continued to believe God, regardless of his circumstances. As a result, his faith became the cornerstone of God's message to all generations.

James 2:23 tells us the high position that God gave to Abraham: Abraham "was called the friend of God." We should eagerly grasp every opportunity to be God's friend. Every time we face a difficult circumstance, it is a God-given opportunity.

Have you ever wondered why a family has a child with serious disabilities? God didn't cause this heartache, but He did allow it. Suffering often wraps these families with a special bond of love that other families never experience. God has permitted them to be thrust into a painful and difficult role in which their faith must stretch. Every day they are challenged to believe that He is working something good. Throughout eternity they, too, may be honored by God for the righteousness they earned by their persistent faith. They, too, may become "God's friends."

At times, prayer may seem to be a journey into unknown territory. We know we are supposed to pray, but we may be tempted to think, *Is this doing any good?*

As I thought about Abraham's journey of faith, I recalled my old restlessness when I tried to pray. Dozens of times I was interrupted with thoughts about all the "important" things I had to do that day. When I finished praying, I wondered if the time was well spent, or if I should have used it in serving the Lord in some tangible way.

The fleshly mind is crafty in its ability to make decisions that seem right but end up being more favorable to the flesh than to the spirit. For example, we can say to ourselves, "I will show real faith in God. I will say each morning, 'Lord, I trust You to meet all of my needs today. To prove my faith in You I will not bother You again today. Amen.'" Then we can get on with our business and feel at ease since we are "trusting God." When we pray, the flesh will devise countless reasons for us not to pray.

Prayer may be at first only a declaration: "God, I know You are there, and I will keep talking to You." Every moment we talk with Him is one of showing our believing.

At times, our prayers should manifest intense zeal. Jesus showed this in Luke 22:44: "And being in agony, He prayed more earnestly. Then His sweat became like great drops of blood falling down to the ground."

In the Old Testament, men often prayed with intensity. For example, Moses said, "And I fell down before the LORD, as at the first, forty days and forty nights; I neither ate bread nor drank water, because of all your sin which you committed in doing wickedly in the sight of the LORD, to provoke Him to anger" (Deut. 9:18). Moses believed that God was listening to him, so he kept praying until he received an answer.

James 5:17 tells us: "Elijah was a man with a nature like ours, and he prayed earnestly that it would not rain; and it did not rain on the land for three years and six months."

God hasn't designed prayer as a form of punishment, which I had sometimes felt it to be. Prayer is our perfect opportunity to learn how to enter His presence.

A Measure of Faith

Throughout the Bible are many illustrations of what happens when people learn to believe God. Do you believe what the Bible says about faith? I don't mean, "Do you understand it?" You can believe in the power of faith even if you don't understand it.

We know that each of us does have faith: "God has dealt to each one a measure of faith" (Rom. 12:3). We must learn how to use what we have.

Positive thinking says, "I can do all things." Eventually that leads to a brick wall. Faith in Christ says, "I can do all things through Christ who strengthens me" (Phil. 4:13).

A man at Lystra had never walked. He heard Paul speak, paid attention, believed God, and did what Paul told him to do. Paul said, "Stand up!" The man leaped to his feet and started to walk (Acts 14:8–10).

Another man who had never walked asked Peter for money. Peter said, "In the name of Jesus Christ of Nazareth, rise up and walk." The man's feet and ankle bones were healed (Acts 3:1–10).

You might think, *If Peter or Paul were here to help me, I could believe.* They aren't here, but that is why God preserved their words so you and I could learn. Their words cry, "Stand up! Don't wait for someone else's faith to help you. Use the faith *you* have!"

I challenge you to use your faith in a way that is so simple you may wonder why you never thought of it. You may never have felt able to believe that you were 100 percent free from sickness or other physical problems. No matter how hard you tried you would still feel the problem.

Peter and Paul didn't ask the men to feel better. They told them to stand up. I'm not asking you to feel better, because feelings often cannot be trusted. I'm suggesting that you take a completely different route.

Try to believe whatever you can believe. Believe that you have twice as much joy as you did yesterday. You can do it! Believe that you can be a better person than you were yesterday. Ignore what your mind naturally wants to feel. Look at what you believe is God's gift to you through Christ. He came to give us His righteousness.

Reach out as far as you can. Believe you are stronger—or even twice as strong. That will be using the "measure of faith" that God has given you.

When I practice using the small amount of faith that I do have, I feel a new surge of strength, and I know that is exactly what God promised to do for everyone. Those who hope in the Lord will

- renew their strength.
- soar on wings like eagles.
- run and not grow weary.
- walk and not faint (Isa. 40:31).

When I'm scheduled for what promises to be a hectic day, and I allow myself to feel hectic, nothing seems right. But whenever I believe God is using that day to bless me and complete His plan for me, my strength and joy leap upward.

Sometimes I feel tired and discouraged. I want to just sit under a shade tree and ignore all my responsibilities. If I give in to these feelings, I will eventually become a tree bearing no fruit and one that God will cut down. I want to be excited over the opportunity He gave me to "fight the good fight of faith" (1 Tim. 6:12).

When life or situations seem to hold you down, don't give

in to the feelings. Claim your God-given rights. I've often wished that God would disregard my lack of faith and work miracles for me, but I know that He wants us to learn to use the faith He has given us.

Jesus Was Excited

Consider the incredible potential that we have of causing every event of every day to create joy in us. Stress, strain, and past fears can be forced to bring new happiness.

Jesus often spoke in parables that were difficult to understand. When asked why He did that, He said some people were not ready to understand. In recent years I have become eager to understand John 7:38: "He who believes in Me, as the Scripture has said, out of his heart will flow rivers of living water." Like many people, I've usually looked for fun, entertainment, and satisfaction from things outside myself. I didn't understand the power of this Scripture.

While attending a special feast, "Jesus stood and cried out, saying, 'If anyone thirsts, let him come to Me and drink'" (John 7:37). When Jesus said those words, He was obviously excited. He knew we could receive something from Him that would be like living water flowing out of us. Water was precious in that day. Jesus offered a fantastic new blessing to anyone eager to understand Him.

The Bible uses a form of the word *joy* 201 times. Joy is a major part of the Christian gospel, yet it often has too small a place in Christian living. Everyone wants joy, but most folks don't know how to revel in it. Many people seek only happiness, and that is a poor substitute for the joy that caused Jesus to be so excited.

The inner joy that comes up like a gusher never depends on

᭏ᴸᴬᵀ other people do or don't do to us. Think of that. What a relief! What a way to live!

In Philippians 4:7, Paul wrote about something that was alive in him. He called it "the peace of God, which surpasses all understanding." This "peace" is so magnificent that Paul could describe it only as beyond "all understanding." Don't be upset with yourself if you don't understand it, but don't give up on learning how to live in it. Circumstances should not control joy. Understand this and life takes on a completely new game plan.

From Acts 13:52 (AMPLIFIED), we learn that "the disciples were continually filled [throughout their souls] with joy and the Holy Spirit." Faith creates joy, and that is God's objective for you and me.

It's tragic that so many Christians think God has deserted them if they aren't healthy, prosperous, popular, successful, and loved by spouses, children, and friends. If you seem to have nothing working for you, you could still be one of God's most treasured children.

I'm serious. It's true. Don't believe people who try to put you down. They may be sincere, but they are dead wrong. Nearly every person in the Bible had severe problems. Even so, they were the people God used.

Be God's person: "Shout to God with the voice of triumph!" (Ps. 47:1). No matter what is happening to you, declare your victory—to Him, to yourself, and to people around you. God will honor your declaration.

"Delight yourself also in the LORD, and He shall give you the desires of your heart" (Ps. 37:4). That sounds pretty good to me. Be delighted in whatever God permits to happen and the rewards are unlimited. Job said, "He will yet fill your mouth with laughing" (Job 8:21). And Romans 14:17 speaks of the "righteousness and peace and joy" of the kingdom of God.

When we realize that God's joy cannot be decreased by our situations, we are then free indeed. In our everyday living there may be situations in which we feel completely helpless—when there is nothing we can do. That is when we are most likely to be afraid.

Every day I hear from men or women whose spouse has broken marriage vows or deserted them. They are devastated and feel betrayed. Often they are bitterly angry or they wish they could die. Does faith in God work in these situations, or should they merely sink into a quagmire of fear?

Ready for the Unexpected

My life has proven to me that I want to build my faith so I will be ready for the unexpected. In 1952, I awakened in a hospital bed. The bed had bars on all sides, reaching—it seemed—about four feet above the mattress. As my mind began to function, my first thought was, *Where am I?*

I had no memory of leaving home or of being ill. My head hurt so badly that I didn't want to lift it off the pillow. I saw words printed on the pillow that gave the name of the hospital and the place as Chicago, Illinois. My home was hundreds of miles from Chicago. How did I get to Chicago? Nothing in my life had prepared me for that moment.

My next thought was, *How could I be somewhere and not know where I am? I must be in a hospital for the insane!* My heart began to beat so wildly that it felt as if it would push through my chest.

In a very weak voice I began to say, "Help, where am I?" No one responded. "Help! Help! Help!" Still no response.

Afraid? Yes, I was really afraid. There is no male, macho, reserve strength for moments like those. What I needed was an inner reserve of faith that would have kicked in at that moment.

After what seemed to be an eternity, my childhood friend, Frank Wigton, walked into the room. He later told me that he had been with me all night as I went in and out of delirium.

"Frank, where am I? What has happened to me? Why am I in this hospital for the insane? Why are these bars all around me?"

"You aren't insane, Merlin. You were in an automobile accident while you were driving here to see me. You had my name and phone number with you so the police called me last night after they brought you here. The bars are only to keep you from falling out of bed."

Frank lowered the bars on one side and held my hand. Tears still come to my eyes as I remember the peace that came to me as my dear friend grasped my hand. My fear melted in the presence of a friend who loved me.

Since then I've learned the blessed reality of the peace that fills the troubled breast when we know that Jesus is holding our hands in even the most difficult situations: "I am with you always, even to the end of the age" (Matt. 28:20). What a glorious reality to live in and abide in!

My unconsciousness and my headache were caused by a concussion, but I was soon able to leave the hospital. That was forty-four years ago, but I still have no memory of driving to Chicago.

Since that day, I, too, have stood at the bedside of many people who had no memory of how they ended up in the hospital. Some were the victims of accidents or war injuries. Others had heart attacks or strokes. And I've ended up in the hospital with other severe problems. But since that fearful day many years ago, I've learned how to keep building my faith so that when the unexpected happens, my faith takes over and destroys the fears that try to control my thoughts.

CHAPTER 14

Steps of Faith

If we pray, "God, heal me," and there is no immediate change in our health, God hasn't forsaken us. He wants us to stand firm in our faith. Hebrews 11:37 speaks of those who were stoned, slain with the sword, destitute, or tormented, yet God gave them a good report. He considered their faith to be righteousness.

Some may say, "What good does it do to have faith if I still have to suffer?" Paul answers that question when he tells us about God's attitude toward these believers: "God is not ashamed to be called their God" (Heb. 11:16).

However, people who do not have faith in God stir His anger:

The LORD said to Moses: "How long will these people reject Me? And how long will they not believe Me?" (Num. 14:11).

Anger also came up against Israel,
Because they did not believe in God,
And did not trust in His salvation (Ps. 78:21–22).

Unbelievers want deliverance now, not later. They want clear, convincing evidence before they will believe. Thomas said that until he saw Jesus' hands and feet, he would not believe He had been resurrected. To Thomas, that may have sounded like clear, rational, levelheaded thinking. But later Jesus said to him, "Thomas, because you have seen Me, you have believed. Blessed are those who have not seen and yet have believed" (John 20:29).

"He appeared to the eleven as they sat at the table; and He rebuked their unbelief and hardness of heart, because they did not believe those who had seen Him after He had risen" (Mark 16:14). And Jesus said to them, "O foolish ones, and slow of heart to believe in all that the prophets have spoken!" (Luke 24:25).

All of us want to enter the world of miracles, but we don't like to endure the day-by-day wilderness journeys in which we have to put one foot painfully in front of the other without knowing where we are going or why. We cannot enter a spiritual world that we don't understand until we learn to walk by faith in the world we do understand. Jesus said: "If I have told you earthly things and you do not believe, how will you believe if I tell you heavenly things?" (John 3:12).

Most of us think if God would do miracles for us, it would be so much easier to have faith in Him. In John 4:48, Jesus gave a stern lesson: "Unless you people see signs and wonders, you will by no means believe." He wasn't at all pleased with those to whom He spoke.

Where Is the Water?

Throughout the Old Testament, God repeatedly blessed men and women who had the boldness to trust Him no matter how long they had to wait for the answers to their prayers. Noah had no evidence that there would be a flood, but he believed and acted on what God told him to do.

For around one hundred years Noah and his three sons worked day after day, building a boat 450 feet long, 75 feet wide, and 45 feet high. The dimensions give a picture of the enormous project that faced Noah. Not only was the proposed boat huge, but there was no water on which to float it. One hundred years of building an enormous structure that seemed to have no value required faith. In those years Noah was the laughingstock of many, but in Hebrews 11:7, God honored him as the man who became "heir of the righteousness which is according to faith."

In those one hundred years (36,500 days) Noah might have asked himself thousands of times, "What good will all this work accomplish? Where is there enough water to float this monstrosity?" Nevertheless, he kept cutting trees and laboriously making them into boards. First he had to find the tree and cut it down. Cut it down with what? He had no power saw or any saw. His only tool would have been a crude ax, possibly made of stone. Now that is hard work! I wonder how many smashed fingers he had during those years? He had to cut the tree lengthwise. Talk about work! It might have taken days to make one board. Then he and his sons had to carry the boards to the building site.

Each one had to be crafted to fit its position, then joined to other boards. Joined how? He had no nails, so he probably designed wooden ones. Then, each seam had to be carefully waterproofed.

I emphasize these points because our faith needs to be patterned, shaped, and designed by the word *persistence*. All the steps of faith have the same name—persistence.

Every day, perhaps every hour, Noah was required to reaffirm his faith that God would somehow use his labors to accomplish something. But what? I can hear Noah saying,

'Okay, God, You must have some good reason for all of this, so I'll keep working."

Noah's steadfastness caused him to be listed in God's Hall of Fame, and he became an example for us to follow. God listed him in the eleventh chapter of Hebrews as one of His heroes.

As I studied that chapter, my attitude toward many things changed. Each situation became a God-given opportunity to trust God. I saw that as the only way I could ever please Him. I repeat, "Without faith it is impossible to please [God]" (Heb. 11:6).

Jesus repeatedly encouraged us to have faith, and He promised us great rewards if we would learn. He said, "Did I not say to you that if you would believe you would see the glory of God?" (John 11:40); and "He who believes in Me, as the Scripture has said, out of his heart will flow rivers of living water" (John 7:38).

Paul wrote about "the exceeding greatness of His power toward us who believe" (Eph. 1:19). I've realized that during those times when my faith in God was weak, I usually did not give myself to prayer. Prayer is an expression of faith, and if I have little faith, there is little incentive to pray. Time spent in prayer is time saying, "God, I believe in You, and I trust You."

God Is Making Me Well

What happens when we try our best to believe God, and our faith is still weak? Consider the child whose father places her on a table and says, "Jump. I'll catch you." If the child is frightened, the father doesn't become angry. He moves a little closer and encourages the child again. The child becomes more confident in her father and joyfully leaps into his arms.

As we continue to say, "Father, I trust You," our faith increases. We must keep making steps of faith. For example, if we have a cold, it's easy to think, *I feel bad now and will probably feel even worse later on.* But if we think, *I feel bad now, but God is making me well,* our faith has an opportunity to grow.

When we trust Him, the Holy Spirit rewards us with great joy, happiness, and inner strength.

At times I hear the ugly voice of this world's god. It says, "Merlin, you are sick and weary." If I listened, my day would be ruined. I would accomplish nothing worthwhile. So I say, "Enough of that; be silent. I'm busy with God's work and will not listen to your lies." Then I begin to thank and praise God, which fills my mind with trust.

The following verse causes some people to be fearful and even question their faith. They think that if this verse is true, they must not be Christians: "If you can believe, all things are possible to him who believes" (Mark 9:23).

Notice that Jesus said "if." That suggests to me that there will be times when we do not have the faith to receive things that we would like to have. What might cause us to be in that condition? John 15:16 gives us one answer: "Go and bear fruit, . . . that whatever you ask the Father in My name He may give you." That makes me believe that bearing certain fruit is necessary in order to receive some things from God. If there is some area of my life in which I do not want to do God's will, I may not be bearing the fruit that He requires of me. And He may require me to do something that He would never ask of you.

In the most difficult circumstances Jesus refused to use His enormous power to do things for Himself. When He was on the cross, the scoffers said, "Descend now from the cross, that we may see and believe" (Mark 15:32).

Most of us would have used whatever power we had and

shown those scoffers a thing or two. That's exactly why we need to do more walking in the wilderness!

Over the years, God has helped me to learn many principles regarding the joy and strength we receive when we praise Him for everything. I know that when I practice believing God, His power works in me. He continues to tell me, "Keep believing, son!"

We all have the same potential that Abraham had. Consider Romans 3:22, which discusses "the righteousness of God, through faith in Jesus Christ, to all and on all who believe." We are part of an elite crowd of believers if we behave the way Noah, Abraham, Isaac, and a host of others did. They showed us the way.

Tough Decisions

Once I had to make a decision that could have a lifelong impact on two people. Whatever decision I made, one person would be hurt. Previously I might have wrestled for days with my dilemma. I saw that the situation offered a good opportunity for me to walk by faith, so I thanked God for the opportunity. Then, instead of endless struggling with the problem, I asked God to give me wisdom and made the best decision I could.

Whenever the matter comes to mind, I use each occasion as a step of faith: "Father, You will protect the person who was hurt and make my decision work for that person's good." Peace returns, and I go on to solve other problems.

More About Noah

Noah saw that the men around him were becoming increasingly evil. He undoubtedly wanted to do something to save his family from what he saw. But what could he do? He was only one man, and the people around him were not interested in what he had to say. Noah heard God saying, "A great flood of water is coming, Noah."

"A flood? What is that?"

"Water will cover the whole earth so that everyone will die."

Noah might have said, "But, Lord, there isn't that much water anywhere. How can that possibly be?"

"Just believe Me, Noah, and do what I tell you. You and your family will be saved."

Noah believed, and he went to work.

One man, Abraham, believed, and the nation of Israel was born. Out of it came Moses, and through him God's law was made known. Out of Israel came Jesus.

What will happen through you and me as we learn to believe God? Our potentials are unlimited! God is still looking for men and women who will make the decision to believe Him and to keep on believing Him regardless of what the evidence seems to be.

Abraham didn't just believe; he acted as if he believed. One step at a time and one day at a time, he did what he thought God wanted him to do.

God has told us that this world will be consumed by fire. You and I have been told to build our "ark of safety." Our ark is formed by our faith. Learning to believe is at least as difficult as building an ark. Noah had never seen one, but he labored on, doing the best he knew how.

You and I do not know how to believe God as completely as Jesus did, but we can help our faith to grow. It requires commitment. Today is the best day we will ever have to begin. Let's believe God is healing us, giving us all the strength and energy that we need, meeting all our needs, using us to prepare the way for the return of His Son, giving us the ability to tell all the world the good news of the gospel.

I'm still hearing the same message: "Merlin, Abraham believed Me, and I counted his believing as righteousness."

CHAPTER 15

Angels Among Us

I stood at the foot of my father's hospital bed. At twelve years of age, I never thought that he might not be coming back home.

"Merlin, be a good boy." Those were his last words to me before someone ushered me out of the hospital room.

A short time later his heart stopped, and the attending physician gave him a shot to stimulate it. Mother told us that Dad opened his eyes and said, "That won't be necessary. I'm going now."

In a few seconds he raised himself to a sitting position and looked toward the foot of the bed. With a radiant smile on his face, he said, "Look, they've come for me!" Then he fell back, dead.

I tell you this to share something that only recently came to my attention. My father's death was sixty years ago, yet it took all this time for the Holy Spirit to help me realize an important detail.

The angels appearing at the foot of my father's bed were in the exact spot on which I had stood only minutes earlier. Why hadn't I seen or felt anyone there? Were those angels at the foot of the bed when I had stood there?

Years later, when my father's mother was dying, another

strange event happened. Grandmother motioned for me to come close, and she whispered in my ear, "Merlin, don't miss it."

"Miss what, Grandmother?"

"The music! The music!"

She heard music, but I heard only her whispering. Why could she hear it, but I couldn't?

These are not isolated incidents. Thousands have heard dying people speak of things they could see and hear. Why do people near death often see and hear things that the rest of us do not?

For centuries, Christianity has taught us that God is omnipresent—everywhere. If so, He is right beside you today. If He is there beside you, why can't you see Him or feel Him?

The Bible teaches us that there may be all kinds of things around us that we don't see:

> *And when the servant of the man of God arose early and went out, there was an army, surrounding the city with horses and chariots. And his servant said to him, "Alas, my master! What shall we do?" So he answered, "Do not fear, for those who are with us are more than those who are with them." And Elisha prayed, and said, "LORD, I pray, open his eyes that he may see." Then the LORD opened the eyes of the young man, and he saw. And behold, the mountain was full of horses and chariots of fire all around Elisha* (2 Kings 6:15–17).

So, at this moment we are probably surrounded by things we can't see or hear. That interests me.

Why don't we see and hear things in the spiritual realm around us? Were human beings always so oblivious to things not a part of the physical world? Are there things we could do that would open our eyes and ears to the unseen world?

The writers of the Old Testament did not consider it relevant to explain how they heard God speaking to them. They heard and they recorded page after page of His exact words. Jesus often quoted the Old Testament, confirming that it contained God's words.

What is still happening around us that we do not see?

Have you ever worked on a puzzle for hours and been baffled by a seemingly missing piece? Then someone walked by, picked up that very piece, and said, "Oh, here's a piece for your puzzle."

Life is like that. One person finds one piece of a spiritual puzzle, while another discovers something that no one else in her generation has understood.

I now am finding pieces to the puzzle of life that for much of my seventy-two years have escaped me. If I can show you where a few pieces fit into your puzzle, then you can go on to find even more during your lifetime. I pray that your adventure will be as exciting as mine. The more I see and hear, the more inspired I am to learn even more.

Moving Toward Our Destination

This brings me to a piece that recently fell into place in my puzzle. I say "fell into place" because I didn't find it. Figuratively speaking, the Holy Spirit looked over my shoulder and brought the following questions to my mind: *Why did my father see things that no one else in his hospital room could see? Why did Grandmother hear music that I could not hear? Why have thousands of people come back from deathbed experiences and reported similar experiences?*

I have come to a much clearer understanding that the

physical body is the temporary home for the eternal spirit. Humankind was corrupted when Adam and Eve sinned, so God drew a curtain between us and what we could see and hear in the spiritual realm. But as this physical body is in the process of dying, the curtain lifts.

Death is seldom instantaneous. The heart flutters; the flow of blood decreases; the body begins to die. The spirit is being released for its journey into the spiritual realm.

But the spirit does not make a geographical journey, for there are no such things as space and distance in eternity. The spirit is released into a realm that you and I do not see.

This is the first time I've ever had the experience of getting old, so much of what I am learning is quite new to me. But it seems that as my natural body moves toward its destination, my spirit is becoming able to see, hear, and understand new things. As my father was dying, his spirit was able to see a different world right there in the hospital room. Years later when she was dying, Grandmother heard music that filled the room.

Moving toward physical death is not the only way to see more of the spirit world. First John 2:15 tells us: "Do not love the world or the things in the world. If anyone loves the world, the love of the Father is not in him." I once saw that verse as being somewhat negative: "Don't do fun things or God will punish you." Now I see it as a positive exhortation to help us find the best things.

The Holy Spirit whispers in my ear: "The things of this world that you see and hear and feel can keep you from seeing into the spiritual world." It seems that nearly everything that the flesh loves can be the means of keeping us from seeing and understanding spiritual things. Money, success, fame, pleasure—the list could go on and on. Jesus tries to help us understand that we can enjoy this life to the absolute maximum if we turn our backs on things cherished by the flesh. He wants to help us, but for much of my life I thought His ways were quite a burden to bear. I wish I had long ago understood His words: "For My yoke is easy and My burden is light" (Matt. 11:30).

Getting older seems to have many disadvantages, but I have a word of encouragement for you from Joel 2:28: "It shall come to pass . . . that I will pour out My Spirit on all flesh . . . your old men shall dream dreams." Sometimes my dreams teach me new things.

In one dream I saw a young man who was deeply in love with a young woman. When he tried to talk with her, she moved away. But the young man wasn't upset. Three times that happened and each time the girl avoided him. Then he said, "I know you don't want to talk with me, but I don't understand why."

"I don't trust you."

"That's all right. God has given me a great love for you, and all I want is for you to be happy. Someday He may give you a great love for me. Please know that I would never do anything to hurt you. If you need my help for any reason, please let me know."

In the dream the man was perfectly content for the young woman to go her way; all he wanted was for her to be happy.

When I awoke, I prayed for understanding.

God loves us and wants to communicate with us. But when we prefer not to have fellowship with Him, He will not force Himself on us. He knows how much He could help us, but He wants us to *want* His presence. Often we are afraid to trust Him because we think He wants to make life difficult.

Reactions to Faith

Have you ever realized how completely our bodies react to what we believe? If you were sure that a murderer was pounding on the door, trying to get into your home, how would you react?

Your heart would beat faster. Your stomach, skin, muscles, and probably every nerve in your body would react. What you believe is important.

What if a supposed intruder pounding on the door turned out to be a close friend? The heart, stomach, skin, muscles, and nerves would have no reason to be upset. They reacted to what you believed at the time.

Faith acts in exactly the same way. The body reacts to what you believe.

If you learn to trust God, your faith can defeat your fears. Do not wait until some great danger threatens before you learn to practice trusting God. Why not learn with everyday little things?

A tiny battery charger I had used only a few days earlier was nowhere to be found. A search through twelve boxes in our garage produced no results.

The next day I spent an even longer time searching through boxes, behind boxes, under shelves, and anywhere I might have placed the charger. By then I was tempted to be afraid I wouldn't find it, and I would have to buy a new one. Then I thought, *Now is the time to rejoice and believe that God is using this to bless me.*

The next day I searched again and kept saying, "Thank You, Lord. You are using this to bless me. There is no reason to be afraid that I've lost the charger. All I need to do is to praise You."

That didn't produce the lost item, so I continued to pray, "Lord, if You want me to find this thing, You could easily tell me where it is. But if not, I will keep on being glad."

A thought suddenly came to my mind: *Look in the trunk of the car.*

The battery charger had never been in the trunk of my car. *There is no reason for it to be there,* I thought. *Oh, well, I'd better look.* And there it was.

What if the charger had not been in the car? I was in a win-win situation. If I hadn't found the lost item, I would have bought a new one, believing that God was using the entire incident for my good.

Each time we learn to trust Him, the stronger our confidence becomes. Believing that God is in control of small matters prepares us to have faith when we have major problems.

Stress is nearly always based on fear. Peace of mind is based on our faith that God is in control of our situation. Jesus said, "Peace I leave with you, My peace I give to you; not as the world gives do I give to you. Let not your heart be troubled, neither let it be afraid" (John 14:27).

Having peace of mind over a lost battery charger isn't colossal, but what if we learn to have faith in many situations every day? To me it's worth learning, and I strongly recommend this way of life. God doesn't want us to be afraid of anything, big or small, and He will help us if we will make the effort to learn how to trust Him.

I have come to believe that what I have is exactly what I need. If I need the spiritual exercise of dealing with an irritable person, God will send that person to me. My purpose in life is not to judge that person or to be upset. It is to believe that God is using the person to bless me.

What great relief that discovery gave me! It's helped so much that I pray you will understand the principle and put it to work for you. Then an irritable spouse, child, or other family member, or a rude driver or shopper, will work for you. Even your boss can be made to work for you.

On the other hand, if we prefer to be irritable, cross, afraid, or to feel harassed by our fellow human beings, God will allow us to hurry our physical bodies on to their demise. Fear is so powerful that if we take it into our hearts, it can quickly gain mastery over health and happiness.

Life can seem eternal until we experience the first symptom of aging. A little ache or pain here and there gets our attention.

The thought comes, *Will I ever become like those older people?* We try to ignore it, but it won't go away. Eventually fear works its way into our thoughts: *What will happen to me? Will I become disabled? Will I end up in a hospital for people who are old and dying?* Such fearful thoughts can work destructively even when we are still young.

Fear says, "If you do this or that, you might lose your health. If you get up early to pray or try to fast or serve the Lord too strenuously, that might shorten your life."

Jesus advised us to live as if we had already lost life. It's gone. We don't have it. But in losing life we have it. Our health then belongs to God, and because we have given it to Him, Satan can't take it away. Our faith gives us the ultimate weapon over all of Satan's devices.

Jesus told God, "I have finished the work which You have given Me to do" (John 17:4). Why should He stay longer? Why should you or I live any longer than to finish our tasks? If we serve God, He alone determines when it is time for us to depart this earth.

Unite with me in learning how to have the kind of faith that defeats fear. Believe me, we will need it. Whatever one's age, now is the time to learn how to be victorious over fear.

CHAPTER 16

When God Says "Don't Do It" He Means "Don't Do It"

Unseen germs cause most of our diseases. These enemies of health went undetected for hundreds of years when the most educated physicians operated with no knowledge of germs. The scalpel might have been wiped with a towel between operations, but that was it. Countless people died.

Louis Pasteur (1822–95), French chemist and microbiologist, proved that microorganisms cause disease, and that each microbe derives from a previous one; one feeds on the other. Invisible bacteria have killed millions.

A "spiritual germ" is also unseen, yet it can defeat every one of us if we do not protect ourselves. This "germ" is also passed from person to person.

God told Abraham that he would be the father of a great

nation that would live in the promised land. But after hundreds of years, that promise had still not been fulfilled.

The Israelites were slaves in Egypt for four hundred years. Generations might have sat around evening fires and wondered if God's promise would ever be a reality.

Nearly five hundred years after Abraham received that promise, Moses finally arrived in Egypt to lead the people out of slavery. They were on their way to the promised land!

As always, God's promise of deliverance was conditional. The people had to trust Him. But they didn't. Instead, they complained again and again.

Paul looked back on their failure to trust God and gave a stern admonition in 1 Corinthians 10:10–12 (TLB):

> *Don't murmur against God and his dealings with you, as some of them did, for that is why God sent his Angel to destroy them. All these things happened to them as examples—as object lessons to us—to warn us against doing the same things; they were written down so that we could read about them and learn from them. . . . So be careful. If you are thinking, "Oh, I would never behave like that"— let this be a warning to you. For you too may fall into sin.*

I am afraid God's "object lesson" has been ignored. We can "behave like that" if we don't know what the Israelites did that caused them so much trouble. We can be involved in their sin of complaining, justified in what we do. That sin can lie undetected as it works its destruction. At times it causes Christians to feel powerless and defeated, and we wonder why we feel so discouraged. That's why Paul tells us to think about what happened to the Israelites, so we don't do the same thing.

God wanted Abraham's children to live in peace in their promised land. But they lived and died in the desert because they refused to trust Him along the way, day by day. He wants Christians today to dwell in our promised land, but for us it is an attitude. Our rebellion can keep us in a spiritual desert.

Paul recognized that Christians of his day were making dreadful mistakes. They were rebelling against God in the same way that the Israelites had. Paul warned Christians not to respond with, "Oh, I would never behave like that."

A few days after the Israelites had marched triumphantly out of Egypt carrying the spoils of God's mighty deliverance, they faltered. They did something we should avoid doing at all costs. We won't unless we understand what the hidden spiritual germ is.

There was no water to drink. Who was in charge of providing it? Well, who had led them out into the desert? Moses. It was his fault!

The people growled and complained to Moses. "Give us water!" they wailed. "Quiet!" Moses commanded. "Are you trying to test God's patience with you?" (Ex. 17:2 TLB).

They might have thought, *What does God have to do with it? Moses is the one who led us out here to die.*

Moses insisted that they were speaking not against him but against God. That's curious, isn't it? They complained to a man, but in God's eyes they were speaking against Him.

But, tormented by thirst, they cried out, "Why did you ever take us out of Egypt? Why did you bring us here to die, with our children?" (Ex. 17:3 TLB).

They were saying, "Don't you even care about our little children?" They were angry and probably afraid. It's easy to clothe our complaints by saying our concerns are for children or older, poor, or sick people. But our complaints are usually centered on, "See what's happening to me, my family, my friends."

The people of Israel argued against God and tempted him to slay them by saying, "Is Jehovah going to take care of us or not?" (Ex. 17:7 TLB).

Why did God prevent them from finding water? He knew that after three days the people would soon begin to die. God knew the problem, but He had some reason for denying water to about three million people. What was that reason? Perhaps His objective was quite simple.

With the millions involved, some might still have believed in the Egyptian gods. They might have needed to be eliminated. When the people continued to grumble and complain, God reminded them of what they had asked Moses in Exodus 17:3: "Why is it you have brought us up out of Egypt, to kill us and our children and our livestock with thirst?" In Numbers 14:28–29, He said, "Just as you have spoken in My hearing, so I will do to you: The carcasses of you who have complained against Me shall fall in this wilderness, all of you who were numbered, . . . from twenty years old and above." His decision revealed that complaining about water or any of our everyday problems isn't the innocent thing we would like to think it is.

All the adults, except Caleb and Joshua, died in the desert. They would never enter the promised land; five hundred years of waiting and hoping were wiped out. We may consider the punishment unreasonable—disproportionate to the offense. Should our failure to trust God be punished by a life sentence without parole?

The sentence of death for eating a piece of fruit in the Garden of Eden may also seem unfair. Our sinful minds usually refuse to accept that disobedience to God should be so severely punished. We can find some reasonable excuse for our actions. But we are cautioned in 1 Corinthians 10:10 (TLB): "Don't murmur against God and his dealings with you, as some of them did, for that is why God sent his Angel to destroy them."

For His own reasons, God allowed the Israelites to be without water for three days. Going three days without liquids causes severe problems. The people suffered and needed help. But more than anything they needed to learn to trust God. That might be the reason that He held back His supply. Eventually He gave them plenty of water, but by then the people had already proven that they wouldn't trust Him to do what He thought was best for them.

They didn't like it when their diet consisted only of manna. Three times a day, seven days a week, nothing but manna. Think a moment about your reactions to life situations. Would you respond as the Israelites did?

"Oh, that we were back in Egypt," they moaned, "and that the Lord had killed us there! For there we had plenty to eat. But now you have brought us into this wilderness to kill us with starvation" (Ex. 16:3 TLB).

How often have you grumbled about the things you had to eat and drink? You probably didn't grumble against God. You probably grumbled against people or your situation without realizing that God permitted you to be in that predicament.

Faith is exactly the opposite of grumbling and complaining. Faith says, "God is in charge of everything, and He is working out everything for my good." If we believe God is using something for our good, we show the quality of faith that He looks for.

.en unpleasant things happen, we would do well to
m.. .tate on Ephesians 5:20 (TLB): "Always give thanks for
everything." We don't like to believe that such a command is
necessary. We often prefer to make our own judgments of
what is permissible in our case.

The Bible honors Abraham for his unusual faith: "Abraham
believed God even though such a promise just couldn't come
to pass!" (Rom. 4:18 TLB). The King James Version says he
"against hope believed in hope."

If we have no money, if friends and family desert us, if we or
a loved one is in pain, it might seem that God isn't working in
our situation for our good. For years, Abraham saw no evidence that God would fulfill His promise. But Abraham
refused to doubt: "Abraham never doubted. He believed God,
for his faith and trust grew ever stronger, and he praised God"
(Rom. 4:20 TLB).

Abraham not only didn't doubt; he was fully persuaded: "He
was completely sure that God was well able to do anything he
promised" (Rom. 4:21 TLB).

As Romans 5:3–5 tells us,

We can rejoice, too, when we run into problems and trials
for we know that they are good for us—they help us learn
to be patient. And patience develops strength of character
in us and helps us trust God more each time we use it until
finally our hope and faith are strong and steady. Then,
when that happens, we are able to hold our heads high no
matter what happens and know that all is well (TLB).

The Israelites believed that their problems and trials would
not work for their good, so they looked for someone to criticize. They lost their chance of a lifetime to learn to trust God
no matter what happened.

Jesus said, "Don't criticize" (Matt. 7:1 TLB). But when we see the flaws in other people, we often think, *Let me help you get that speck out of your eye.*

Jesus had a one-word reaction to anyone who was critical of others: "Hypocrite!" (Matt. 7:5 TLB). A hundred times each day we have the opportunity to criticize others. After all, we reason, they need it.

During my seventy-two years on the earth, I have criticized many people. I have even criticized the same person many times. As I look back I realize that about 99 percent of the time my criticism did not help the persons. Instead, my criticism ended up hurting me.

On the other hand, I've been criticized often, and I can't recall once when it made me feel good or helped me to become a better person.

When you are criticized, don't be upset because even Jesus was criticized. Others found fault with Him when

- He ate with people of ill repute (Mark 2:16).
- His disciples didn't fast (Matt. 9:14).
- He worked on the Sabbath (Matt. 12:10–11).
- He let people crowd around Him when He hadn't taken time to eat (Mark 3:20–21).
- He went to sleep when the disciples needed Him to keep the boat afloat (Matt. 8:24).
- He said a dead person was only sleeping (Luke 8:52).
- He let His disciples eat without washing their hands (Mark 7:5).
- He permitted unholy people to touch Him (Luke 7:39).
- He let people waste money on Him (John 12:5, 7).
- He called God His Father (Matt. 26:65–66).

Romans 14:13 urges, "Don't criticize each other any more" (TLB). Some Christians may believe they have received a special anointing from God to find fault with other folks. Somewhat like "Card-Carrying Criticizers." But James 4:12 asks, "What right do you have to judge or criticize others?" (TLB).

How about your spouse? Even if that person is nearly perfect, you could still find many opportunities every day to criticize. If you give in to that urge, you will move farther into a spiritual desert.

James 5:9 declares, "Don't grumble about each other" (TLB). We will remain anemic, weak, and powerless until we learn how to stop being critical of others. There will always be people, living and working with us or around us, who need to improve. Always! Why are they there? We need them!

They supply us with exactly what we need. The Israelites didn't believe that, so they criticized Moses. They didn't get away with it, and neither will we.

Criticism is like germs. It takes everything that is bad in us and makes it worse. Every time we find fault with people or God, we move ourselves farther into the desert. And like the Israelites, we will stay there until we learn—or die.

Yes, the Israelites were still God's children even after they disobeyed Him. For forty years He miraculously supplied their food, water, and clothing. They still couldn't enter the life God had planned for them. You and I will remain children of God, and we may think that we are living a Christian life, but we will not receive many of His promised blessings until we learn to obey Him. Like it or not, that's the way it is.

Praising God for everything that happens to us causes us to enter a deep, satisfying, restful trust in God. We believe that all of life's bitter, painful experiences are used by God for our good to produce His peace in us. And that is the foundation for living in incredible joy.

A chemist can take a poisonous ingredient and modify it until it becomes a healing medicine. God wants us to take the evil things that attack us and compel them to help us. Why should anyone resist His incredible offer?

Job 5:17 states, "Happy is the man whom God corrects; therefore do not despise the chastening of the Almighty." Each of us needs to learn how to be that happy man or woman. We can, once we learn to believe that God keeps His promises. As our faith rests on His joy, our joy becomes incredible!

CHAPTER 17

Power-Works

Joshua—what a man!

To understand power and how it works, consider Joshua. While others were complaining, he was learning. Living in the wilderness—on a one-item diet—caused millions of people to complain. But Joshua did the unusual; he kept his mouth quiet. And God selected Joshua to lead His people.

Remember the mustard seed–sized faith we discussed earlier? Joshua showed the incredible power that you and I could have if we helped that tiny seed of faith to grow. Joshua spoke to the Lord in the presence of the Israelites:

> *"Sun, stand still. . . ."*
> *So the sun stood still,*
> *And the moon stopped,*
> *Till the people had revenge*
> *Upon their enemies. . . .*
> *The sun stood still in the midst of heaven, and did not hasten to go down for about a whole day* (Josh. 10:12–13).

Did that really happen? Yes, it's as real and trustworthy as God's Word.

Think of it. What had to happen for the sun to stand still?

The universe is designed to move, and it is held together by the laws of gravity. Billions of stars swirl through space, and each depends on the gravitational pull of all the others. When the sun stood still, something awesome had to happen.

Joshua probably knew nothing about gravity and the forces of the universe, or about the motion of the earth. He didn't need to. He had learned to believe that God would take care of it—whatever needed to be done.

Though Joshua did not realize the awesome power needed to stop the sun and moon, that didn't affect God's willingness to act. The event reveals God's willingness to move heaven and earth to solve any problem that we have.

So what if every known law has to be changed?

So what if our problems seem great?

So what if our faith seems weak?

If you and I believe that God will take a problem and make it work for our good, God will use His awesome power to reward our trust in Him.

If He has to change people or situations, present or future events, is that any different from what He did for Joshua? So what if He has to take an evil scheme that Satan devised and make it work for our good?

I began to examine some of my own prayers. Sometimes the prayers themselves revealed that I didn't believe God would answer them.

Here is an illustration. I prayed, "God, please help me to feel better" with a complaining ring in my voice. There was nothing wrong with my words, but the tone of my voice said, "I don't believe He will help me feel better." If you had heard me pray in that discouraged manner, you would have known that I didn't really expect God to help me. So my prayer left me feeling depressed.

Then I tried to say my prayer over and over until the tone in my words reflected joy and conviction that God *would* help me. My prayer did not sound "doubting and double-minded." Please experiment with a prayer of your own and see if you can make it sound as if you really expect God to answer. I believe you will be pleased as you see prayer and faith taking on a new and happy meaning. As your attitude changes from one of fear to one of believing, you will eventually experience new delight.

We must practice prayers that we believe are being heard and answered. If our faith is too weak to ask for a giant miracle, we should ask for things we believe God will do. Instead of saying, "God, please give me perfect health," we may need to say, "I ask You to bring healing to me. Yes, God, I really do believe You are healing me." That's a mustard seed–sized faith that can grow day by day until it has the power that will move anything.

Jesus said, "Whatever things you ask in prayer, believing, you will receive" (Matt. 21:22). Notice He said, "Ask in prayer, believing." He emphasized the importance of believing while we are asking.

In Mark 11:24, He said, "Therefore I say to you, whatever things you ask when you pray, believe that you receive them." I have seen this principle working when people have asked me to pray for them. If their problem was severe, my heart often strained, anxiously hoping that God would heal them. But when the problem was that severe, I had a question mark in my prayer. It's extremely difficult not to be anxious when you see a huge problem staring you in the face.

Sometimes I have prayed for people without knowing anything about their problem. My prayer held no doubt or uncertainty. And at the same time I sensed the Holy Spirit was quickening my heart with confidence. I somehow believed that God was answering their prayer. Miracles were reported at those times when there was no doubting.

Remember all the Bible characters who grew in faith? They didn't see immediate answers to big prayers, but they kept asking, in faith believing.

Luke 2:52 reported, "Jesus increased in wisdom and stature, and in favor with God and men." Think of that. Even Jesus had to increase in favor with God. He increased by His daily obedience to God. You and I can also increase. If we are willing, we can learn how to honor God's promises.

Incredible power—it belongs to those who are eager and willing to do whatever is necessary to grow in faith. God's gift of faith is alive in us. We can learn to use it to defeat any doubts or fears that may lurk within us.

The absolute certainty that your Creator hears and is answering your prayers will be one of the most satisfying, exciting, and enjoyable experiences you will ever have. Jesus assured us, "I give you the authority . . . over all the power of the enemy" (Luke 10:19). That's incredible!

CHAPTER 18

Have No Fear, Joy Is Here

People often ask me why there seems to be a discrepancy between praising the Lord for everything and claiming God's promises. I know that God uses both methods to help many people.

I was on my early morning prayer walk when a fresh understanding came into my spirit. I wasn't thinking about the two approaches for receiving God's promises, but the Holy Spirit filled my heart with this comprehension: faith and trust in God grow in each person's heart in different ways, just as the same seeds grow differently in various soils. Some folks fix their attention on Bible verses that promise healing, and they receive healing. Others fix their attention on believing that God will provide them exactly what He knows is best for them, and they receive healing.

God isn't concerned with *how* we grow in faith; He is concerned that we do it. No procedure is perfect because human beings put methods into practice. Whatever approach we use, God is pleased if we come to the place where we trust Him more. And I want to do whatever I can to help you live a life of faith in Christ so you will always be moving away from fear toward faith.

Some people face problems that you and I may never encounter, but our goal is the same. We must learn to have the kind of faith that works, whatever the situation. I was recently drawn into circumstances in which I wanted to help men who had a different kind of problem from any I had ever had.

What happens when a man becomes so afraid of what may happen tomorrow that he cannot deal with today? He sometimes contemplates suicide. Unless he finds a solution to his problems, he may eventually end his life.

Lloyd's of London is the giant insurance company that is in the business of insuring million-dollar projects. Worldwide natural disasters during the 1990s have caused the firm to lose a reported twelve billion dollars.

Executives in British corporations are often individually liable for corporate losses. Many directors of Lloyd's of London are said to have lost their homes and everything they owned. All of the men had been fabulously wealthy. Losing everything caused a reported thirty-two executives to be so afraid of the future that they took their own lives.

One of the directors read my book *Prison to Praise*. He was so impressed that he had his secretary contact me to see if I could come to London and speak to the other directors.

On the appointed day, I stood in a magnificent mahogany-paneled study, facing an audience of impeccably dressed businessmen. They appeared to be eminently successful, except for their faces. They looked utterly miserable. Maybe they were upset that they were required to waste time listening to this American when they could be busy taking care of important business matters. For whatever reason, they appeared to be most unhappy.

I spoke with all the enthusiasm and joy that I could muster. I used illustrations that usually bring smiles to the audience. Nothing worked. My audience grew increasingly downcast. My joy seemed to be making them even more resentful.

Lord, what can I do? Please help me. I'm wasting my time and theirs.

Then I heard an inner whisper, *Teach them the song that I taught you.*

I thought, *Oh, Lord, I must be misunderstanding You. Surely You don't want me to teach them that song. They won't understand! They will think I'm really stupid.*

But I received no further guidance. The only thing I could do was to stop my planned message and ask, "How many of you know the song 'London Bridge Is Falling Down'?"

The men glanced at one another. They were obviously baffled. *What is this idiot doing now?* No one made any effort to answer my question.

So, the only thing I knew to do was to sing the little song the Lord had taught me. It was to the tune of 'London Bridge Is Falling Down':

God is working for my good, for my good, for my good.
God is working for my good; yes, He really is.

As I sang, I saw a slight smile on one man's face—ever so slight. Then I said, "Please sing with me." And off I went again:

God is working for my good . . .

No one sang, but I saw more smiles; tension began to melt from their faces. So, I sang it again. By the time I was through nearly everyone was smiling. Something had happened. The men were hearing me!

God often uses childlike things to accomplish His purposes. Remember David's attack on Goliath? David used a slingshot, and he won the battle. David said to the Philistine, "You come to me with a sword, with a spear, and with a javelin. But I come to you in the name of the LORD of hosts. . . . The LORD will deliver you into my hand . . . that all the earth may know that there is a God in Israel" (1 Sam. 17:45–46).

When I switched back to my message, I had a new audience. They listened to me. When I was finished, three of the directors told me they wanted copies of *Prison to Praise* to send to Lloyd's of London offices all over the world.

Please listen to me, dear reader. That little song is true. It's true for me, and God wants it to be true for you. He wants us to trust Him. He gave us the instrument of faith that we can use to claim victory over every kind of fear.

Since that day in London, I've been teaching that same song to thousands of people. Many of them report remarkable changes in their lives as they sing it and believe it. Physicians and psychologists have been teaching it to their patients. One psychologist told me that for months she had been trying to help an especially depressed patient. After the doctor read about this song in our monthly *Praise News,* a free newsletter that Mary and I send out every month, she taught it to the patient and prescribed that the patient sing it many times every day.

The following week the patient returned with her husband. He wanted to thank the doctor for the remarkable change that had taken place in his wife. The healthy change has continued.

Make that little song a way of life for yourself. God will use it to melt fear from your heart and strengthen your faith in His promises. It may seem silly, but if it works, why knock it? Sometimes I change the words to these:

God, You're working for my good, for my good, for my good.
God, You're working for my good; yes, You really are.

If I don't feel faith stirring in my heart, I sing it again and again until I do. Then I quote Romans 8:28: "All things work together for good to those who love God." Lord, I want to love and trust You. I'll keep singing and believing. Sooner or later my heart begins to sing. Anxieties flee as my heart goes from fear to faith.

It is difficult to be upset about anything if we really believe that God is working for our good. That is why Joseph could so freely say to his brothers: "You meant evil against me; but God meant it for good" (Gen. 50:20).

Mary and I take great delight in seeing God work out difficult situations as we sing, "God is working for our good." I strongly recommend that you adopt this song as your own. Sing it as if it were absolutely true (and it will be). I promise you that God will use it to rekindle childlike happiness in your heart.

CHAPTER 19

Maturing in Faith

If our faith remains fragile, we will live in a shadow world of sometimes believing God and other times wrestling with doubts and uncertainties. We desperately need to grow in faith in order to be better prepared for the last days—just prior to the return of Christ. These days will be more stressful than most of us have ever experienced. Natural disasters, such as earthquakes, will increase in all parts of the world.

In the future we may lose all electrical power and gasoline. Within days or even hours, medical help could be minimal to nonexistent. Sources of food and water could be gone within hours. If the thought of losing these things brings fear to your heart, think of what the actual experience could do!

Regardless of how well our families or friends are doing, fear can give us a relentless uneasiness that something is wrong. Fear that lies hidden in our hearts can make us feel that we must do something more to protect our loved ones from unseen dangers. The Bible tells us that the wise person anticipates trouble and prepares for it (Prov. 22:3). But God has also told us to trust Him and never be anxious over these concerns. God's enemy wants us to fear that some unknown tragedy is just around the corner. Those kinds of fears will live in us unless we learn how to increase our faith.

Peter experienced a phenomenal miracle when he walked on water, but for some reason his fear was stronger than his faith. When he saw the waves, he sank. You and I may be in a state of physical prosperity and emotional stability, with everything going our way. But if we have not learned how to defeat fear, we are not prepared for the future.

The key is to believe that *whatever happens* is a God-given opportunity for us to trust Him. If Peter had understood that, instead of being afraid he could have shouted, "Hey, Jesus, here comes a big wave! Are we going for a swim?"

Quick References

The Bible is filled with many exhortations against yielding to fear. Here are just a few of them. Keep them handy for quick reference when some wind of adversity blows in your direction.

When you are tempted to think that God is not concerned about the needs of your children:

The angel of God called to Hagar out of heaven, and said to her, "What ails you, Hagar? Fear not, for God has heard the voice of the lad where he is" (Gen. 21:17).

When you are tempted to be afraid of suffering that might come when you choose to do the right thing:

But even if you should suffer for righteousness' sake, you are blessed. "And do not be afraid of their threats, nor be troubled" (1 Peter 3:14).

Never think that you are not important enough for God to protect. We can all claim the promise that He gave:

If you are Christ's, then you are Abraham's seed, and heirs according to the promise (Gal. 3:29).

Never be afraid that God will leave you because of your weakness:

[The Lord] is the One who goes before you. He will be with you, He will not leave you nor forsake you; do not fear nor be dismayed (Deut. 31:8).

Do not be afraid because of the strength of the opposition:

He said, "Listen, all you of Judah and you inhabitants of Jerusalem, and you, King Jehoshaphat! Thus says the LORD *to you: 'Do not be afraid nor dismayed because of this great multitude, for the battle is not yours, but God's'"* (2 Chron. 20:15).

We should not fear what other people can do to us:

Do not fear those who kill the body but cannot kill the soul. But rather fear Him who is able to destroy both soul and body in hell (Matt. 10:28).

So we may boldly say:

> *The* LORD *is my helper;*
> *I will not fear.*
> *What can man do to me?* (Heb. 13:6).

Do not be afraid of the rumors spread by the news media:

Lest your heart faint,
And you fear for the rumor that will be heard in the land
(A rumor will come one year,
And after that, in another year
A rumor will come,
And violence in the land) (Jer. 51:46).

Do not fear that God's good news is not for you:

The angel said to them, "Do not be afraid, for behold, I bring you good tidings of great joy which will be to all people" (Luke 2:10).

Do not fear, little flock, for it is your Father's good pleasure to give you the kingdom (Luke 12:32).

Maturing in faith accomplishes three things.

First, it pleases God: "Without faith it is impossible to please Him" (Heb. 11:6). And He is pleased when we believe without requiring physical evidence, as stated in Hebrews 11:1: "Faith is . . . the evidence of things not seen."

Second, it makes us happier and helps us feel that our lives have accomplished something worthwhile.

Third, it helps us to give blessings to others. Every day I receive hundreds of letters and many telephone calls from people who thank me for helping them to find their way out of difficult problems. My faith journey has helped them, and they in turn encourage me. And I'm inspired even more to seek out those who have not yet learned how to help their faith to mature.

Faith is somewhat like a cup of hot coffee (or your favorite beverage). Picture yourself on a bitter cold evening walking through fierce, freezing winds and then arriving home. Someone hands you a steaming hot cup of your favorite beverage. You eagerly clasp the warm cup and feel its warmth triggering plea-sure in your cold hands.

At that point do you have the warm cup? Yes, you have it, but it still is not in you.

You can have a kind of faith that you cling to but has not yet made its way into your heart. You want to believe, and strive to believe, but confidence eludes you.

Now imagine the difference that you feel when you drink the hot beverage. Now you really have it. It creates a warm glow in you, just as Romans 5:5 reminds you: "The love of God has been poured out in [your heart]."

Maturing faith creates a warm glow of confidence that God is working through you to accomplish His purpose. This faith abides in you and does not require that you strain to receive its benefits. In fact, the more you strain, the less effective your faith may be!

One illustration stands out in my mind. Mary and I were at a Korean church in New York. When I invited those who want-ed to be prayed for to come forward, hundreds moved toward the front of the church. The pastor organized them into a line, and the people waited patiently for Mary and me to pray with each person and family.

There were so many people wanting prayer that it seemed we prayed for hours. Around 1:00 A.M. the last family stood before us—a man, a woman, and a teenage boy. I was so tired that I didn't ask what they wanted us to pray about. Since we did not know what they wanted, I made a simple prayer for God to meet whatever need they had. But as I prayed, I knew God had met their need. I cannot explain exactly how I knew, but when that confidence comes, I've learned to recognize it.

Later that morning we were scheduled to have breakfast with the pastor. We were surprised to see that same family accompanying him. They did not speak English, but I could tell they were quite excited about something. The pastor explained it to us. They had waited so long to be prayed for because their need was so great. Their teenage son was scheduled for surgery to remove an orange-sized cancer from his knee. When they returned home after our prayer, the son said, "Look at my knee!" The cancer was gone!

Can you imagine how thankful I was that God had given us the privilege of praying for that family? Can you understand why I am so passionately interested in doing whatever I can to help my faith to mature? Do you understand why I am so eager to encourage everyone to do whatever possible to grow in faith?

In closing, I speak to those of you who have never seen or experienced a miracle. You may be tempted to feel like a second-class Christian. Don't!

What is a mighty, powerful faith? You and I may want faith that moves mountains, cures cancer and arthritis, or eliminates pain in a loved one. That kind of faith is needed, but I think God's favorite faith is outlined in Hebrews 11. Those saints had strong enough faith to believe God even though some of them never received in this life what God had promised. Abraham must have been God's favorite example, and he died before all of God's promises to him were fulfilled. Abraham refused to doubt. When you and I also refuse to doubt, we become God's future stars.

We can mature in faith in everyday affairs. A friend loaned Mary a tiny convertible sports car. Mary fell in love with it and wanted one of her own. My instant response was, "Never! They are too dangerous. I don't want to lose you."

Mary was patient with me, but I could tell she really wanted a small car. She wasn't concerned about its age, color, or make: "Just a small convertible, Merlin."

Did I dare have the necessary faith to believe God would protect her? Did I have that much faith? Would my faith presume on God's grace? It was one big problem for me.

Finally I had to realize that God loves Mary more than I do, and that I needed to trust her to His care. She got her Fiat convertible, she enjoyed it immensely, and God watched over her. But it was not a one-time opportunity for my faith to grow. Every time Mary pulled out of our driveway I was tempted to be afraid. I could imagine her being crushed between two trucks or smashed by a reckless driver or sliding upside down during an accident. Satan loves to project all kinds of tragedies into our minds, and he will do so unless we learn to resist him. Over and over I had to renew my confidence in God's loving care. He gave me the opportunity because He saw that I needed to mature in my faith.

Remember to practice using faith. Practice believing that you are the happiest person in the world, even if your emotions tell you it isn't true. God honors whatever you believe. Go for a walk and believe that every step takes you one step closer to heaven. Practice believing until faith overcomes your doubts. Believe that the righteousness of Christ is His gift to you not because of your goodness, but because of His goodness. Practice believing that every breath you breathe increases your health and joy.

Think, believe, and declare victory in Christ—victory like winning the championship. Victory over every problem and every disease. But what if you die, as we all will eventually? Here is the answer: "Death is swallowed up in victory" (1 Cor. 15:54).

When you step from this life into the next, God will roll out the red carpet. You will have fought the good fight. You will have kept the faith.

About the Author

Merlin Carothers, author of *Prison to Praise*, is well known throughout the Christian community. His books have sold more than 15 million copies and have been translated into 37 languages. A Master Parachutist, he served in the Eighty-second Airborne Division during three major campaigns of World War II and then as a guard to General Dwight D. Eisenhower. Later he became a Lt. Colonel in the U.S. Army Chaplaincy. He is a pilot, author, lecturer, pastor, and evangelist. He has made many appearances on national television and travels worldwide to share what he has learned. Carothers lives with his family in San Marcos, California.